The Grammar Guide

An introduction to the structure of English
and the words we use to describe it

John Seely

The Grammar Guide is an ideal introduction to grammar for *everyone* who
wants to know more about the structure of the English language – including
primary and secondary school teachers and older students. In fact, the Teacher
Training Agency recommends it to primary school trainee teachers:

subject knowledge for
Primary English

Heinemann

Halley Court, Jordan Hill, Oxford OX2 8EJ

A division of Reed Educational and Professional Publishing Ltd

OXFORD MELBOURNE AUCKLAND
JOHANNESBURG BLANTYRE GABORONE
IBADAN PORTSMOUTH (NH) USA CHICAGO

02 01 00

10 9 8 7 6 5 4 3

ISBN 0 435 10197 8

Designed by 320 Design

Printed and bound in Great Britain by
Biddles Ltd, Guildford and King's Lynn

Contents

Introduction

Using this book

Studying language is all about **levels**. To begin with, you need to be sure that you know the level at which you want to study it. As its name suggests, this short book is a guide, a brief introduction for readers who have little or no background knowledge. It is not for people who can cope perfectly easily with explanations at this level:

> "In Old English, nouns distinguished five cases – nominative, accusative, genitive, dative, and instrumental – though the distinction between dative and instrumental was neutralised inflectionally and other distinctions were often neutralised in particular declensions..."
>
> Sidney Greenbaum: *The Oxford English Grammar*

Greenbaum was writing a definitive grammar of English in 600+ pages. His definitions had to be watertight. It should be very difficult to find sentences that are not accurately described in his analysis. To achieve this he wrote at length and in great detail.

The *Grammar Guide* has only 112 pages. Inevitably it has to simplify. There are bound to be omissions – things left out because they are too complicated, or too rare to be included in such a short account. This guide will have succeeded if, after reading Part A, and referring to Part B, you come away with a clearer understanding of the structure of the English language and the words we use to describe it.

The structure of the book

Part A is an introduction and explanation. It is written to be read through. As new ideas and words are introduced they are explained in brief and you are referred to the page(s) in Part B where you can find more detailed information. Part A is less than fifty pages long and it should be possible to read it through in one sitting.

Part B is designed for reference. If you want to know more about how verbs work, for example, then Part B will explain them in more detail than is done in Part A. You can find them by using the detailed index at the back of the book. Between the end of Part B and the beginning of the index there is also a Glossary containing brief explanations of all the main grammatical terms used elsewhere in the book.

How you use the book is up to you. If you find the very idea of grammar challenging, possibly even intimidating, then it would be a good idea to begin by reading Part A. If you just want a 'quick fix' on a particular topic, then the Glossary or Part B would be a more logical place to start. The publishers and I have tried to make the interrelationships between the parts as transparent as possible. If you have comments or suggestions, we should be grateful to receive them.

Part A: Understanding grammar and language

1 Grammar and communication

Levels of language

When we come to analyse how language works we soon find that we have to study it at several different levels simultaneously.

Imagine you are in a foreign country. You turn on the radio. A stream of sound comes out. You can identify that it is a human voice and you think it is making speech sounds – as opposed to music, for example. Beyond that you cannot make head or tail of it. You assume it is a language of some kind, but you have no way of knowing this. It is just a stream of noise. You don't know which of the sounds you are hearing are significant and which are completely incidental – the result of the speaker having a cold, or a regional accent, for example. You twiddle the radio tuner and hit upon a different station. Again you hear speech, but this time the language seems vaguely recognisable: there is a vocal 'tune' that seems familiar and you can distinguish certain vowels and consonants. That 'th' sound could be Spanish, perhaps? You retune the radio again. This time the sounds are definitely familiar and you can begin to pick out one or two words: 'mezzo', and 'bella'. You can't work out what the speaker is saying, but you recognise the language as Italian. On the next retuning you encounter someone speaking French and while you cannot understand everything she is saying you get the gist: it is a weather forecast and the area where you are staying is in for heavy storms for the next 48 hours.

Phonemes

Such an experience is not uncommon and provides a good starting point. Language is a means of communication that works through sound. (Or by making visible marks on paper, a computer screen, or whatever, but for the moment we will focus on speech.) The stream of speech sound can seem very variable, but in fact there is only a limited range of sounds that make a difference to meaning. English speakers can hear that the word 'cat', for example, contains three sounds: c - a - t. Different speakers may actually pronounce the three sounds slightly differently (especially the vowel), but they recognise that there are just three significant sounds. If we change just one of these we either get a different word (eg 'bat') or a nonsense word (eg 'zat').

These significant sounds are called phonemes. English has 44 phonemes. These are divided fairly evenly between vowels, which are sounds made with the mouth and other speech organs open and unobstructed, and consonants, which involved some closing of one or more speech organs.

Intonation

In addition to phonemes, English also communicates through intonation, the 'tune' of the sentences. You can say the words, 'David has gone' as a statement, with your voice falling at the end or you can make it a question by letting your voice rise at the end.

Stress

Finally there is stress. We can pronounce certain syllables with greater force. Words of more than one syllable always have one syllable that is stressed more than the others. This 'comes naturally' and is essential to communication. (Try saying the word 'examination' with the stress on the first syllable, for example. It's difficult to say and difficult for others to understand.) As well as word stress there is sentence stress. The statement, 'David has gone' can be said with any of the three words stressed more than the others. Each version conveys a different meaning. Try them:

David has gone. (ie '...but only David.')

*David **has** gone*. (ie 'Don't disagree – I'm telling you.')

*David has **gone***. (ie 'I just can't believe it – he's...gone.')

So the first and most basic level of language is that of sound: phonemes, intonation, stress.

Words

The next obvious level is that of words. We form sounds or letters into fairly short groups called words that have identifiable meanings. A competent English speaker can see that this sentence has not been written down correctly:

Weformsoundsorlettersinfairlyshortgroupscalledwordsthathave identifiablemeanings.

In writing we use spacing to separate words. Speech does it in ways that are more complex, partly through stress and intonation. Most English speakers don't find it difficult to grasp the concept of the word.

We sometimes refer to the store of words available to us as our 'vocabulary'. Linguists often prefer to call it 'lexis'. Whichever term you use, the store of words available to an individual is an important measure of his or her linguistic ability.

That personal vocabulary can be divided into active and passive. Your passive vocabulary consists of all those words you recognise and broadly understand when you come across them in speech or writing. Your active vocabulary is smaller and contains those words you are comfortable using.

Morphemes

There is, however, an intermediate level between phonemes and words. Compare these two sentences:

She has lost her book.

She has lost her books.

Although only one very slight change has been made, the two sentences have very different meanings. In the first, only one book is missing; in the second it is more than one. The 's' we have added to 'book' has changed the meaning of the sentence.

Changes like this are called 'morphemic' and the 's' that indicates plural is called a morpheme. A morpheme is the smallest unit of language that conveys meaning. So 'book' and 's' for plural are both morphemes. The study of how words are changed to alter meaning is called 'morphology'. Two important areas of English morphology are the formation of the plurals of nouns and the formation of the different forms of the verb: 'walk'/'walks'/'walking'/'walked'.

So we have these three levels:

WORDS
↓
MORPHEMES
↓
PHONEMES

Grammar

But of course we don't use words in isolation, as a series of separate thoughts or references to the real world. There is a limit to what we can communicate through a single word. Take an archetypal foreign language situation: the foreigner in a country whose language he cannot speak. He just knows a few words. He is starving. He goes up to a market stallholder selling various fruits and says, 'Bananas'. The stallholder may understand him to mean 'I want to buy some bananas.' If so, the foreigner is in luck. On the other hand the stallholder may reply, 'Yes, we have some very good bananas today. Do you want the big fat ones from Cameroon or these nice sweet little ones from Jamaica?' On its own 'bananas' communicates very little.

So we have to combine words in order to communicate more precisely. The study of how we combine words is called grammar. We now have four levels:

GRAMMAR
↓
WORDS
↓
MORPHEMES
↓
PHONEMES

What grammar is about and how it works is the subject of the next chapter.

2 Working the system

The four levels that have been described constitute a formal system. In one sense, if you want to explain 'how English works', all you have to do is describe its grammar, lexis, morphology, phonemics and the writing system. What such a description doesn't do is explain **how** English speakers use their own language. How do they choose from the apparently infinite range of vocabulary and sentence structure? If we cannot answer this question then we cannot achieve a comprehensive view of the place of grammar in communication.

In the analysis that follows I shall focus on written language, in the interests of simplicity, but much of the analysis applies to speech just as well.

The five questions

We use language primarily in social situations. The language we use is determined partly by the nature of language itself and partly by how we respond to the situation we are in and what we want to achieve. In simple terms we make our language choices by responding to five simple questions:

What?

Who?

Why?

Where?

How?

What?

The subject matter we are dealing with plays a very important part in deciding the vocabulary we use. It's difficult to talk about a football match, for example, without using words like 'player', 'ball', and 'goal'. This poses few problems unless the language we want to use is technical and possibly unfamiliar to our audience or may put them off in some other way (eg by being considered to be 'jargon'). Then we have to make a judgment.

Consideration of the subject matter has important implications for the text even before the writer puts pen to paper. If we don't define clearly what we are writing about, then we are unlikely to produce a clear and coherent piece of writing. One of the commonest causes for poor writing is just this lack of definition. Once the subject is clearly defined, the writer can begin to create a structure for the whole text – and this applies whether that text is a three paragraph letter or a two hundred page report.

Hand-in-hand with this process of definition goes knowledge of the subject matter. This may simply be a question of ordering information in our mind or on paper, or it may require some research. Again this is something which is best done before starting to write. There is nothing more frustrating for the writer than to discover in the middle of writing the first draft of a text that a key piece of information is missing and unlikely to be available for some time.

Finally the information and ideas which compose the 'what?' must be presented in a clear and orderly way so that however long the document, the reader feels confident and comfortable with it. This again is a matter of planning and organisation.

So, when we answer the question 'What?' we are making decisions about the vocabulary of the text and also about its shape, structure and organisation.

Who?

Most of the writing we do is intended to be read by someone else. There are exceptions, of course: shopping lists, rough notes, and private diaries, for example. Most of the time, however, we write to communicate. So it is important to consider the needs of our audience. There are three questions we need to ask:

• What is their ability as readers?

Age, education, and intellectual ability all contribute to the reader's ability to tackle a text. A text for young children, for example, needs to be much simpler than one for university students. Simplicity is a matter of both vocabulary and grammar. Young readers often find long words difficult and may struggle with a text that contains long sentences with several subordinate clauses. At the other end of the scale, sophisticated readers are likely to be turned off by language that is too simple and babyish.

• What do they already know about this subject?

Readers place a new text in the context of the knowledge and understanding they already have. If the writer assumes too much prior knowledge then readers will be lost; if too much unnecessary background information is provided, then readers will be irritated and frustrated. It is also important to present such introductory information without becoming boring and repetitive.

• What is my relationship with my readers?

Sometimes we write for people we know well; we make assumptions about our relationship and hence about the kinds of language we can use. At other times our audience is completely unknown and we can make no such assumptions. All texts can be placed on this matrix:

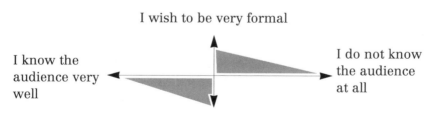

Most texts will fall within the shaded areas, but some will fall outside them. (For example, although the writers of information books for young children don't know their audience personally, they often wish to address them in an informal way.)

Why?

Writers' purposes in writing can be described in many different ways, but these eight cover most situations:

1 to inform

Examples: reports, newspapers (sometimes), reference books

2 to regulate

Examples: laws and regulations, rules of games, recipes, instructions for equipment

3 to persuade

Examples: adverts, project proposals, newspaper leaders

4 to enquire

Examples: questionnaires and forms, some letters

5 to interact

Examples: personal letters, cards and e-mails

6 to entertain

Examples: fiction and poetry, many magazine articles

7 to record

Examples: diaries and other types of journal, shopping lists, notes

8 to hypothesise

Examples: personal notes and writing plans, some letters, some company in-house planning documents

The first four of these are probably the commonest reasons for writing in everyday life. They cover most of the reasons people use writing at work, for example. Much of what we read outside work, however, is designed to entertain and away from work many of us write to interact, for example, when we communicate with friends and family members. The last two purposes listed are different from the rest in that they do not necessarily involve an audience.

Purpose informs the structure, grammar, and vocabulary of the text. If the writer loses sight of this, then all these elements will be weaker. The relationship between purpose and these linguistic elements is not a simple one. Some purposes have obvious links with specific

p23 ▶
p96 ▶
grammatical forms: regulating often involves *imperatives* ('Take the pin in your right hand'); hypothesising uses *conditionals* ('if we do this, then that will happen'); finding out requires questions. Some purposes influence choice of vocabulary particularly strongly: writing that seeks to persuade, for example.

Where?

When we have a conversation with someone, the physical setting can affect how we speak and what we say. Two old friends will probably speak to each other differently in church at a funeral from in a pub late at night. The particular format we use for writing can have similar effects. There are several well-established formats, for example:

- reports

- letters

- feature articles

- essays.

More recently newer electronic formats have established themselves, for example:

- fax

- e-mail.

Each of these formats has a set of conventions concerning structure and presentation. Most also imply certain types of vocabulary and a choice of grammatical structures. The reader comes to expect these and the writer often finds them a useful support – although sometimes the conventions may become irksome and even cause problems of their own. An example of this is the difficulties some have in writing letters to people they don't know personally.

Of course, there are many other formats available to the writer, and it is important to be aware of the conventions, strengths and weaknesses of any format you wish to use.

How?

Most writing we do can be allocated to one or more of these four modes of discourse:

1 Narrative

This includes any writing that relates a sequence of events that happened over a period of time, either in the order in which they happened or in some other order chosen by the writer. Examples include fictional stories, newspaper reports, and some aspects of other reports.

Narrative makes heavy use of key grammatical features such as *past tenses* and other time markers ('then', 'the next day', and so on), and *temporal clauses* introduced by connnectives such as 'while', and 'when' (eg '*After they had gone*, *we stayed talking for a while*.') ◀ p77 ◀ p95

2 Description

Description takes in any account of what something or someone looks, tastes, feels, sounds or smells like. Whereas narrative generally covers a period of time, description is often either in the present or at one specific point in the past (or, sometimes, the future). Many information books contain passages of description (for example, a guide to garden plants), so do a variety of forms of travel writing, and it is common in magazine and other feature articles as well as a range of technical writing.

Description is not so clearly tied to grammatical forms as narrative, although as suggested above, it can often take place in the present. On the other hand it is difficult to write good description without the ability to construct and control extended *noun phrases* (eg '*She was an elderly, frail-looking woman with silver-grey hair*.'). ◀ pp 33–35, 73–75

3 Exposition

This seeks to explain a state of affairs, how something works, what an organisation, situation or set-up is like. Description is largely concerned with appearances, whereas exposition goes below the surface to enquire and describe the workings of something, whether physical, like a car engine, or social, like a transport system. You will find examples of exposition in a wide variety of texts, including information books, technical pamphlets, newspapers and magazines.

Exposition is likely to involve more sophisticated ways of thinking and writing than narrative and description. In particular, it is difficult to write effective exposition without the ability to use and control a pp92–96 ▶ variety of *complex sentences*.

4 Argument

The essential feature of argument is that it states a position and provides some kind of reasoning for it. It is thus often combined with exposition, since much exposition is not entirely objective, but rather the product of a writer's experience and judgment, which he or she then seeks to justify through argument. A classic example is the newspaper leader or comment column which is either purely argument or largely argument with a small amount of introductory exposition.

Like the other modes, argument has its own distinctive grammar and p95 ▶ vocabulary. *Adverbial clauses beginning with the connective 'because'* are an obvious example (eg *'This was clearly a mistake,* ***because shortly afterwards the bank was forced to raise interest rates again.'****)*

3 Never end a sentence with a split infinitive

Descriptive and prescriptive grammar

Grammar is a way of describing how a language – in this case English – works. It isn't a set of rules in the legal or moral sense. It doesn't tell us what we should or should not do with our language. The rules of grammar are more like scientific laws: attempts to generalise and set out patterns to account for a range of evidence.

Grammarians base their judgments on a corpus, a body of spoken and written material. For example, Sidney Greenbaum's *Oxford English Grammar* uses a corpus called ICE, the 'International Corpus of English'. Greenbaum draws heavily on the British section of this, a set of 500 texts each containing about 2000 words – a million words in all. It includes transcripts of informal conversations, scripted speeches, newspaper extracts, business letters, and a wide variety of books.

Greenbaum uses this corpus to establish and support a series of generalisations about how English works. His book is an excellent exposition of English grammar and if you want to understand in more detail about a specific topic it is well worth referring to. What it will not do is tell you what you ought to say or write.

Prescriptive grammar

So what about these people who say, for example, it is wrong to split an infinitive? On what basis do they say that such usage is 'wrong'? In general they base their judgments on what is sometimes called 'traditional grammar', which in turn leant heavily on a study of Latin.

In the past, it was often believed that by comparison with the classical purity of Latin, English was a poor, corrupt degenerate thing which could only be improved by making it more like Latin. If you described English in terms of Latin grammar then you might be able to 'purify the dialect of the tribe'. For example, Latin verb infinitives are one word (eg 'ire') and are impossible to split, so although English verb infinitives consist of two words (eg 'to go') we should avoid splitting them at all costs. This has no real basis in grammar or logic and can actually cause considerable problems for the writer. Look at this sentence, for example:

> Most of the people he was talking to were too young **to really remember** politics before Thatcher.

If you put 'really' somewhere else in the sentence you actually change its meaning (eg '...*too young really to remember*').

Many of the rules of prescriptive grammar are similar to this, and are honoured more in the breach than the observance. But is this simply to admit that there are no 'rules' and that anything is allowed? Clearly not. Grammar has a lot of straightforward rules that we break only at our peril. For example, if you tamper radically with English word order you risk being thought eccentric or foreign:

> *The verb in a statement sentence normally after the subject comes.*

or you might communicate the wrong message. You would certainly be able to see no difference between these two sentences:

> *The subject precedes the verb.*
> *The verb precedes the subject.*

Why study grammar?

The purpose of studying grammar is to gain a clearer understanding of how real language works. To do this we need to learn how to analyse sentences. This discipline is very valuable. Not only does it make us more effective readers – since it helps with the disentangling of long and complex sentences. It also helps with writing. When we redraft a text we often have to break down long sentences into shorter sentences or combine shorter sentences into longer ones. We also need to compress sentences by reducing the length of certain components. Studying grammar provides a useful training in the analysis of complicated sentence structures. This analytical skill is most useful when we are redrafting our own texts or editing those of other writers.

The terminology, too, is valuable. It is much easier to explain where a sentence is going wrong if one can refer to the relevant parts by their correct names. If a child knows the terminology, the teacher can say, 'The subject and the verb don't agree.' If the child doesn't know – and can't identify – the subject and the verb, then it is necessary to go through a complicated business of analogy and reasoning to get to the same point.

How grammar works

When we talk about language, there is a tension between meaning and form. As far as possible, grammarians define their terminology purely **formally**. They say, for example, that adjectives are words that can be used to modify nouns. Users of language are often more concerned with the meanings we use adjectives to convey. Hence the simple definition of an adjective as a 'describing word'. On the whole such **notional** definitions of grammatical terms don't work very well and formal ones are more accurate. On the other hand we have to be aware all the time of the meanings that different grammatical features are capable of conveying, and it is this communicative approach which will be taken here.

The grammatical hierarchy

Most descriptions of grammar work at four levels: sentence, clause, phrase, and word. This is put most concisely by Sidney Greenbaum:

'❏ a sentence consists of one or more clauses

❏ a clause consists of one or more phrases

❏ a phrase consists of one or more words'.

(Sidney Greenbaum: *The Oxford English Grammar*)

So, the sentence *Aunt Mary had prepared a meal while Peter was resting,* can be analysed as shown on page 22.

Aunt Mary had prepared a meal while Peter was resting.

SENTENCE

Aunt Mary had prepared a meal | while | Peter was resting
CLAUSE | **CONJUNCTION** | **CLAUSE**

Aunt Mary | had prepared | a meal
NOUN PHRASE | **VERB PHRASE** | **NOUN PHRASE**

Aunt | Mary | had | prepared | a | meal
NOUN | **NOUN** | **VERB** | **VERB** | **ARTICLE** | **NOUN**

The rest of Part A will examine in detail how this analysis works – so don't worry if it seems a little complicated at this stage!

4 Seven amazing facts about elephants

Grammar is about how sentences are constructed. Sentences, however, are quite difficult to define simply. One traditional definition is that a sentence is 'the expression of a complete thought or idea'. It is, however, easy enough to think of sentences that are grammatically correct, but which do not fit this definition. For example, what is the complete thought or idea in:

Is that it?

Equally there are plenty of non-sentences that seem to express a complete thought or idea. For example:

DANGER LIVE CURRENT

or

God

It is better to define a sentence in formal terms: as a grammatical unit that consists of one or more clauses.

Sentence types

There are *four types of sentence*:

◀ p89

- **declarative**
  These are sentences normally used to make **statements** like 'Elephants are dangerous'.

- **interrogative**
  These are normally used to ask **questions** like 'Are elephants dangerous?' or 'What are those elephants doing?'

- **imperative**
  These are normally used to make **commands, orders, requests** etc like 'Look at that elephant!'

- **exclamative**

  These are used to make **exclamations** of various kinds such as 'How charming that little baby elephant is!'

Each of these sentence types has a distinctive word order. This chapter is all about word order, so we shall stick to declarative sentences, the type used to make statements, since they are by far the most common.

Five basic clause patterns

Throughout this chapter we'll look at sentences that consist of just one clause, and in the process find out more about what a clause actually is. We'll do this by looking at sentences no more than four words long.

As the chapter title suggests, all the sample sentences are about elephants. If you want to try out the ideas and sentence patterns in the chapter, think of a topic of your own as the basis for parallel sentences. Choose a plural concrete noun (one that refers to a person or thing) – like 'books', 'trains', or 'engineers'. Then use it to construct sentences on the pattern of the 'elephant' ones used as examples.

Subject + verb

The shortest sentence you can make starting with the word 'elephants' consists of two words, for example:

Elephants exist.

This sentence consists of one clause. The clause has two parts, a subject and a verb:

SUBJECT	VERB
Elephants	exist.

The subject

p81 ▶ The *subject* of sentences like this has these characteristics:

- it comes at or near the beginning of the sentence;

- it comes before the verb;

- it is a noun or a noun-like thing (a pronoun or noun phrase – see next chapter);

- it frequently, but not always, gives a good idea of what the sentence is going to be about.

The verb

The *verb* has these features:

◄ p82, 37–43, 60–63, 76–78

- it normally comes immediately or shortly after the subject;

- it agrees with the subject in number ('one elephant walks'; 'two elephants walk') and person ('I am'; 'she is'; 'they are');

- it provides information about an action ('walks') or a state ('believes') or links the subject to another part of the sentence in some other way (as 'am' does in the sentence 'I am happy').

The simple pattern of subject + verb can be used to generate thousands of other sentences. They may have just two words like the sample sentence, or they may have many more:

SUBJECT	VERB
Elephants	**exist**.
Elephants	charge.
Elephants	are starting to charge.
The older bull elephants	are starting to charge.

Although the last sentence has four times as many words as the first, it still has the same two **clause elements**: subject and verb. In the next chapter we'll look at how a single word like 'elephants' can build into a group of words like 'The older bull elephants'. Chapter 6 pays similar attention to the verb.

Subject + verb + object

You can't, of course, make sentences of the subject + verb type with just any old verb. This is not a complete sentence:

Elephants want

The immediate response to that is 'want what?' The sentence is missing a key part: the object. So, our second pattern covers sentences like this:

SUBJECT	VERB	OBJECT
Elephants	eat	grass.

The object

p82 ▶ The *object* of a clause or sentence:

- normally comes after the verb;

p31–36 ▶ - is a *noun or noun-like thing;*

- usually refers to a different person, thing or idea from the subject. (the exception to this is objects that include the part-word 'self' – as in 'I cut myself', where subject and object refer to the same person.

The subject + verb + object pattern can be developed in a similar way to the subject + verb one:

SUBJECT	VERB	OBJECT
Elephants	eat	grass.
An adult bull elephant	can be expected to eat	tons of grass.

Again the second sentence follows exactly the same pattern as the first, even though it has far more words.

Subject + verb + object + object

We have seen that some verbs, like 'want' have to have an object. There is a small group of verbs that normally have not one but two objects, and a larger number that sometimes follow this pattern. This 'sentence', for example, is not complete, even though it has a subject, a verb, and an object:

Elephants give children

We are left asking, 'Elephants give children what?' It is true that 'children' is an object, of a kind; it fulfils all the requirements in the list above. But it still needs a second object:

SUBJECT	VERB	INDIRECT OBJECT	DIRECT OBJECT
Elephants	give	children	rides.

'Rides' is the direct object – it is what the elephants give. 'Children' is the indirect object because the children are the ones who benefit from the rides – the ones that the rides are being given to. You can always tell this type of sentence because it can be rephrased like this:

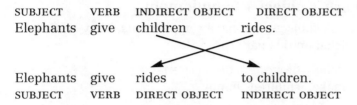

SUBJECT	VERB	INDIRECT OBJECT	DIRECT OBJECT
Elephants	give	children	rides.

Elephants	give	rides	to children.
SUBJECT	VERB	DIRECT OBJECT	INDIRECT OBJECT

Many verbs that refer to the action of passing something from one person or thing to another work in this way. Examples are 'hand', 'pass', and 'show'.

Subject + verb + complement

There is another pattern which resembles the subject + verb + object pattern, but which is actually very different:

SUBJECT	VERB	COMPLEMENT
Elephants	are	animals.

The word 'animals' is a *'noun or noun-like thing'* and it comes after the verb, so we might expect it to be an object. But it fails the other test: it does not refer to something different from the subject. The items before and after the verb refer to the same thing. The sentence is like a mathematical equation:

◀ p31–36

Elephants = animals.

The complement

In this clause pattern the element that comes after the verb provides more information about the subject, it serves to **complete** it, so it is called the *complement,* or more fully, the **subject complement**. It:

◀ p83

- comes after the verb;
- is a *noun (or noun-like thing)* or an *adjective* (as in the sentence, 'Elephants are big.');

◀ pp31–36, pp58–59

- refers to the same person or thing as the subject.

This type of clause uses a special type of verb, called a linking (or 'copular') verb. The commonest of these is 'to be'. Others are 'seem' and 'appear'.

Subject + verb + object + complement

Objects, as well as subjects, can have complements. They occur in clauses constructed on this pattern:

SUBJECT	VERB	OBJECT	COMPLEMENT
Elephants	make	children	happy.

You can contrast this clause with one we looked at earlier:

Elephants give children rides.

It is true that both have two elements after the verb: a direct object and something else. In the earlier sentence, 'children' and 'rides' refer to completely different things. In this sentence, 'children' and 'happy' refer to the same thing. The word 'happy' serves to give more information about the object 'children', it **completes** it. Hence the name **object complement**.

The object complement

This clause element:

- comes after the object;

- provides additional information about the object;

- can be a *noun (or noun-like thing)* – as in the sentence 'They made me secretary', or an *adjective,* like 'happy'.

pp31–36 ▶
pp58–59 ▶

The story so far

We have looked at five basic clause patterns:

SUBJECT	VERB
Elephants	exist.

SUBJECT	VERB	OBJECT
Elephants	eat	grass.

SUBJECT	VERB	INDIRECT OBJECT	DIRECT OBJECT
Elephants	give	children	rides.

SUBJECT	VERB	COMPLEMENT
Elephants	are	animals.

SUBJECT	VERB	OBJECT	COMPLEMENT
Elephants	make	children	happy.

In each of these patterns **every clause element is essential**. If you remove one the structure stops being a clause and is grammatically incomplete.

The missing piece of the jigsaw

There are two other clause patterns which are much less common than the five we have been looking at so far. They only occur with a very small number of verbs, but they are important.

Subject + verb + adverbial

We saw how some verbs need to be followed by particular clause elements. For example, in this pattern:

SUBJECT	VERB
Elephants	eat.

we need an object to complete the pattern. Similarly the pattern 'Elephants are…' needs a complement to complete it. The following sentence opening sets up a similar need:

SUBJECT	VERB
Elephants	live.

This part sentence raises questions such as, 'Elephants live where?' To complete the pattern we need a third element:

SUBJECT	VERB	ADVERBIAL
Elephants	live	here.

Subject + verb + object + adverbial

pp85–86 ▶

There is also a small group of verbs that take an object and then also require an *adverbial*. For example:

SUBJECT	VERB	OBJECT	ADVERBIAL
I	put	the book	there.

You can't have the sentence without 'there'.

Adverbials

pp85–86 ▶

So *adverbials* are the missing piece of the jigsaw, bringing the total number of clause patterns to seven. Unfortunately, as we shall see, adverbials are awkward customers. Although they only crop up in these two 'compulsory' positions in clause patterns, they can appear almost anywhere in any of the other patterns as an optional element:

SUBJECT	VERB	ADVERBIAL
Elephants	exist	now.

SUBJECT	VERB	OBJECT	ADVERBIAL
Elephants	eat	grass	slowly.

SUBJECT	ADVERBIAL	VERB	OBJECT
Elephants	usually	eat	grass.

ADVERBIAL	SUBJECT	VERB	COMPLEMENT
Usually	elephants	are	big.

As can be seen from these few examples, adverbials carry information about when, where, and how the events in the sentence occur. They also allow for more general comments on this, such as 'fortunately'.

pp44–48 ▶ This will be examined in considerably greater detail in Chapter 7.

5 Nouns and noun-like things

We saw in the previous chapter that the subject, object, or complement of a clause could be a noun...or a 'noun-like thing'. In this chapter we have a closer look at nouns and related grammatical features.

Nouns

Nouns are fairly familiar to most people. They can be divided into two groups. **Proper** nouns are the names of individual people, places, organisations, works of art, and so on – all of which usually begin with a capital letter. The important thing about proper nouns is that they refer to things that are one-off. You can only have one John Prescott or Milton Keynes. We mark this special nature by awarding initial capital letters. When official titles are used in this way we give them a capital letter ('The Foreign Minister said...'), when they aren't ('There were several foreign ministers present.'), we don't.

◀ pp56–57

All other nouns are **common.** Some people like to divide them into 'abstract' and 'concrete', but this is more to do with what they mean than how they behave grammatically. A more useful division is into **countable** (or 'count') and **uncountable** (or 'non-count'). As the names suggest, countable nouns can have a plural, normally ending in 's', while uncountable ones cannot. Uncountables include all proper nouns and most (but not all) abstract nouns: you cannot have more than one 'contentment', for example. There is also a small group of concrete nouns that are usually uncountable, mostly things that are thought of in the mass rather than as a set of individual items: sand, mud, ice, butter, and so forth. But beware: almost all uncountables can become countable in special situations. 'The sands of time are running out' is an example.

You might ask whether it matters if a noun is countable or not. The answer is that certain words describing quantity cannot be used before uncountable nouns. These include 'each' and 'several'. Nor can you precede an uncountable with the article 'a(n)'. More important, it is not standard English to use 'less' before a countable plural. It's 'less butter' and 'fewer biscuits'. 'Less' is, however, increasingly used with plurals in informal speech.

To sum up: nouns can be proper or common, countable or uncountable. In addition, as we shall see, they can be turned into noun phrases and can be modified by adjectives.

Pronouns

pp66–68 ▶

Before that, however, there is an important group of words that can also act as the subject, object, or complement of a clause: *pronouns*. It is sometimes said that they are called 'pronouns' because they are used 'instead of nouns'. This is a rather misleading oversimplification. Look at that last sentence. 'This' is definitely a pronoun, but it isn't standing in for a noun. It is referring back to a whole sentence which begins, 'It is sometimes said…'. So, it is more accurate to say that pronouns refer back to something already written or said. This may be:

- a noun;

- another pronoun or group of pronouns;

pp33–35, ▶
73–75

- *a noun phrase* (shortly to be explained);

- a section of text – part or all of a sentence, or even a group of sentences;

- an idea or fact already mentioned.

In addition, you will probably have noticed that we sometimes use 'it' as the subject of a sentence when it refers back to nothing at all. For example:

It is raining.

In sentences like this, 'it' is described as a 'dummy subject' because in effect the sentence has no real subject. 'There' is used in a similar way (eg *'There's a lot of bad weather about.'*)

Types of pronoun

Pronouns come in a range of shapes and sizes, according to use. They are covered in more detail in Part B and are listed here for completeness:

Type	examples
Personal	I/me, he/him etc
Possessive	mine, hers etc
Reflexive	myself, themselves etc
Demonstrative	this, that etc
Indefinite	someone, anyone etc
Interrogative	who, what etc
Relative	who, that etc

Pronouns in use

The best way to get a good hold on how pronouns work is to take that list and read through a piece of prose identifying the different types of pronoun used and the things they refer back to. The biggest problem writers have when using pronouns, as any teacher is aware, is making sure that it is clear what or whom particular pronouns refer to. Writers often use pronouns in a vague or ambiguous way.

Summary: pronouns in clauses

A pronoun can be the subject, object or complement of a clause:

SUBJECT	VERB	OBJECT
I	love	**you**.

SUBJECT	VERB	COMPLEMENT
It	is	**I**.

or, less formally,

It	's	**me**.

Noun phrases   ◀ p73–75

We have seen that a noun can also be the subject, object or complement of a clause. It is relatively uncommon, however, for a noun to stand on its own in this way. More often the noun is the centre or **headword** of a noun phrase. A phrase forms part of a clause. It can consist of a single word (a verb, a noun, an adjective or an adverb) or a group of words built up on a verb, noun, adjective or adverb. In addition, as we shall see, there are prepositional phrases – groups of words that begin with a preposition.

While it is true that you can use the single noun 'elephants' as the subject, you cannot use 'elephant'. 'Elephant eats grass' is not a complete clause; it needs something else, for example:

SUBJECT	VERB	OBJECT
An elephant	eats	grass.

The commonest type of word for this purpose is the **article**: 'a(n)' and 'the'. There are several other words that serve a similar purpose:

this, that etc
my, his, her etc
some, any etc
one, two etc

All these words help to give the noun slightly greater definition, and are called **determiners**.

Modifiers before the noun

Our noun headword 'elephant' can be given a lot more definition, by adding words before it, to **modify** its meaning:

SUBJECT			VERB	OBJECT
A	hungry young bull	elephant	eats	grass.
DETERMINER	MODIFIERS	HEADWORD		

pp35–36, ▶
58–59
The commonest kind of word that can come before a noun to modify it is an ***adjective***. 'Hungry' and 'young' are both adjectives modifying elephant. One way of building up a noun phrase is just to string a number of adjectives together before the noun. (There is more about adjectives at the end of this chapter and in the reference section.)

It is not only adjectives that can come before a noun to modify it. In the example above, 'bull' also modifies the noun. It tells us the elephant is a male. But 'bull' is a noun, and nouns are frequently used before a noun headword to modify it.

Modifiers after the noun

We can also give information to define the noun by placing words after it. For example:

SUBJECT			VERB	OBJECT
An	elephant	in the savannah	eats	grass.
DETERMINER	HEADWORD	MODIFIER		

A wide range of phrases can be used after the noun to modify it in this way. They are detailed in Part B. It is useful to mention one at this stage, in the interests of completeness.

Adjectives

◀ pp58–59

We have seen one very important feature of adjectives: they are placed before a noun to modify it. Most adjectives can be used in this way, which is called **attributive**.

We have, however, seen adjectives being used in another way: as a complement. We can use an adjective as a subject complement. For example:

SUBJECT	VERB	COMPLEMENT
Elephants	are	big.

This use of adjectives is called **predicative**. Most adjectives can be used both attributively and predicatively, but a few are restricted to one or other of the two categories. For example 'alone' can only be used predicatively. We can't talk about 'an alone person'.

Grading

An important way of categorising adjectives is into **qualitative** and **classifying** adjectives. Qualitative adjectives give information about the qualities of the noun they modify. Examples are 'big', 'hungry' and 'expensive'. Classifying adjectives place the noun into a class or category such as 'pregnant', 'annual', and 'western'.

This might seem interesting but unimportant, were it not for the fact that qualitative adjectives can be **graded**. By putting certain words (intensifying adverbs: see p65) in front of them we can comment on how much of the quality the noun has. Compare these three phrases:

an intelligent student
a highly intelligent student
a fairly intelligent student

The use of 'highly' and 'fairly' makes an 'extremely' big difference to the meaning.

You cannot grade classifying adjectives. It would be odd to describe a school prize-giving as 'a highly annual event'. Even so, sometimes people break this 'rule' to achieve a special effect. (For example: *'She was looking very pregnant.'*) The word people make a fuss about is 'unique', a classifying adjective meaning 'the only one of its type'. It is properly objected that it is impossible to have something that is 'very unique'. On the other hand there is nothing wrong with saying that something is 'almost unique'.

Comparison

Qualitative adjectives can have different degrees of comparison:

ABSOLUTE	big	beautiful
COMPARATIVE	bigger	more beautiful
SUPERLATIVE	biggest	most beautiful

Single syllable adjectives and certain two-syllable adjectives add -er and -est. Almost all words of three or more syllables use 'more' and 'most'.

Ordering

As we have seen, it is possible to put a string of adjectives in front of a noun to modify it. English is quite fussy about the order in which the adjectives are placed. We learn this as we learn the language and most native speakers would have no difficulty in identifying that the adjective order in this phrase is wrong:

a wooden grey large house

But, try teaching it to foreign learners! (The general order is:
1 qualitative adjectives, 2 colour adjectives, 3 classifying adjectives:
'a large grey wooden house'.)

6 What is this thing called 'verb'?

We'll begin by revisiting three of the sample sentences from Chapter 4 and seeing how they used verbs:

Elephants exist.
Elephants eat grass.
Elephants are animals.

One of the key features of *verbs* is that they change their form, or '**inflect**' more than other words. Nouns, for example, just have a singular and plural form (and some don't even have that). But look at this:

◀pp60–63, 76–78

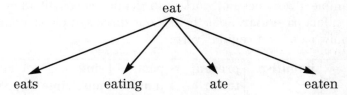

The first thing we notice is that not all of these forms can be used on their own in a clause, we cannot say:

Elephants eating grass.
or
Elephants eaten grass.

and claim that it is a complete clause. Each is missing something. We need to add words:

*Elephants **are** eating grass.*
*Elephants **have** eaten grass.*

The second thing is that we have to make sure we choose the right form of the verb to fit the rest of the sentence. So this, too, is wrong:

Elephants eats grass.

Forms of the verb

The verb has five forms, or parts:

- **stem** (eat)
- **present tense** (eat/eats)
- **past tense** (ate)
- **-ing participle** (eating)
- **-ed participle** (eaten)

We can add to this a sixth:

- **infinitive** (to eat)

Regular and irregular verbs

The example given does not work in the same way as all other verbs. 'Eat' is in fact **irregular**. So is 'be'. Of our three sample sentence verbs, only 'exist' is a **regular** verb:

stem	infinitive	present tense	past tense	-ing participle	-ed participle
exist	to exist	exist exists	existed	existing	existed
eat	to eat	eat eats	ate	eating	eaten
be	to be	am is are	was were	being	been

You will notice that even with a highly irregular verb like 'be', it is still the stem that is used to form the -ing and -ed participles.

Sentence verbs

We saw in Chapter 4 that sentence verbs could be divided into three groups:

Verbs that need an object

We saw that in normal speech, 'Elephants eat...' is incomplete because it leaves us asking, 'eat what?' Verbs like 'eat' that need an object are called **transitive**.

Verbs that do not need an object

'Exist' on the other hand is not followed by an object and is an **intransitive** verb.

It is important to note that some verbs can be both transitive and intransitive. For example 'work':

- *I am working.*

- *He worked his passage.*

Linking verbs

These verbs are used to link a subject and its *complement*. They include 'be', 'seem' and 'appear'.

◀ pp27, 83–84

Other verbs

Another name for sentence verbs is **full** verbs. That is because they are verbs with a 'full' meaning – one that you can look up in a dictionary. (For this reason, linguists sometimes also call them 'lexical' verbs.)

There is also a group of verbs that don't have a dictionary meaning and are not normally used on their own in a sentence. They are used with full verbs. For example:

A

*I **am** eating bread.*
*They **have** eaten bread.*
*You **do** eat bread.*

B

*I **shall** eat bread.*
*I **might** eat bread.*
*I **could** eat bread.*

pp61–62 ▶ All these verbs are called *auxiliaries* because they help full verbs. They have been divided into two groups above, because they have different characteristics.

Primary verbs

The verbs in Group **A**, 'be', 'have', 'do' can also work as full verbs. For example:

> I **am** happy.
> They **have** a new car.
> You **do** woodwork and pottery.

These primary verbs are thus dual function.

Modal auxiliaries

The verbs in Group **B** cannot work as full verbs and normally appear with a full verb. The full list is:

- will, shall, would, should;

- may, might;

- can, could;

- must.

There is a big difference between the meanings of the two sets of auxiliaries. Compare these pairs of sentences:

- *She is working today.*
  She may be working today.

- *You work on Sundays.*
  You must work on Sundays.

Modal auxiliaries create a range of **possible** situations (from 'may' through 'will' to 'must'). The primary auxiliaries deal in **actual** situations.

The verb phrase

The analysis of clause elements in Chapter 3 focused almost exclusively on verb phrases that consisted of just one word. This restricted us to just two tenses, the present and the past. Some linguists only use the term *'tense'* in this way, to describe two contrasting forms of the verb ('eat(s)' and 'ate'). So, they say, English has no future tense. Newcomers to modern grammar find this somewhat disconcerting. What about 'I will eat'? Isn't that the future tense of 'eat'? And if it isn't the future tense, what is it?

◀ p63

A more pragmatic way of looking at things is to use the term 'tense' in a looser and wider way, which is what will be done in this book.

Tense and aspect

We have already seen one form of the present tense:

Elephants eat grass.

English has, however, more than one form of the present tense. For example, compare these two sentences:

*I **eat** breakfast at eight o'clock.*
*I **am eating** breakfast at the moment.*

They are both 'present' in the sense that both describe something that is **true now**. But only the second describes something that is actually **happening now**. We call the first ('eat') the **simple present**, and the second ('am eating') the **present continuous** (sometimes called the 'present progressive'), because it refers to actions that are continuing.

There is also a third form of the present. Compare this sentence with the two previous ones:

*I **have eaten** my breakfast.*

It refers to an event that happened in the past, but the speaker is still thinking about it – its effects (good or bad) are still in his or her mind. So, it is in one sense 'present'. In another sense it is completed – the action has been 'perfected'. Hence the name of this tense, the **present perfect**.

These three versions of the present tense, simple, continuous and perfect are called *aspects*. They allow us to express considerable sophistication through the verb phrase. These three sentences all cover the same facts but in subtly different ways:

◀ p76–77

I live in Esher now.
I am living in Esher now.
I have lived in Esher for some time.

p77 ▶ # The 'tenses' of English

Each of these aspects is available in present, past, and future tenses. Despite the strictures of some linguists we therefore have these 'tenses' in English:

Present

SIMPLE	she lives
CONTINUOUS	she is living
PERFECT	she has lived
PERFECT CONTINUOUS	she has been living

Past

SIMPLE	she lived
CONTINUOUS	she was living
PERFECT	she had lived
PERFECT CONTINUOUS	she had been living

Future

SIMPLE	she will live
CONTINUOUS	she will be living
PERFECT	she will have lived
PERFECT CONTINUOUS	she will have been living

p78 ▶ # Tense and time

Despite the wide range of tenses English has to offer, there are also many other ways in which we can indicate time in our sentences. The simple present tense, for example, can be used to talk about past, present, future and timeless events:

- *This man goes into a pub and says to the barman...* (past)

- *Shearer shoots...It's a goal!* (present)

- *We fly to New York on Thursday.* (future)

- *Water freezes at O degrees Celsius.* (timeless)

Future time, in particular, is represented in a variety of ways:

- *We fly to New York on Thursday.*
  (Simple present used for scheduled actions.)

- *We are meeting her next week.*
  (Present continuous used for plans.)

- *We are going to have a drink together tomorrow.*
  ('Going to' future for plans.)

- *We'll see you on Friday.*
  ('will/shall' future – unstressed future)

It is important to note that in many cases the precise time of an event is shown by a combination of verb phrase and one or more words which indicate time ('Thursday', 'next week' and so on.) These **adverbials** form an important part of the next chapter.

7 Adverbs and other awkward customers

Up to this point we have looked at basic clause patterns and these types of phrase:

- noun phrases
- the verb phrase

plus these word classes:

- nouns
- pronouns
- adjectives
- articles
- verbs.

So, we have made good progress, but we are left with something of a job lot of phrases and word classes to consider.

Adverbs

pp64–65 ▶ *Adverbs* themselves form a job lot (or, as linguists might say, 'a heterogeneous group') that can prove rather difficult to pin down.

pp85–88 ▶ First we must distinguish between adverbs and *adverbials*. An adverb is a single word and adverbs are a word class like nouns and adjectives. An adverbial is a clause element like subjects and objects. An adverbial may be an adverb or it may be something else as we shall see. An adverb can also form part of a phrase.

What adverbs do

It used to be very easy. I was taught at school that adverbs modify verbs, adjectives and other adverbs. To some extent this is true, but it is only part of the story. It is more helpful to divide adverbs into groups according to what we use them for.

By far the biggest group is used to add meaning to the sentence as a whole, to part of it, or specifically to a verb, adjective, or adverb within it. That sounds complicated but should become clearer as we look at these **'adjuncts'** in more detail.

Adjuncts

◀ p65

The bulk of these provide answers to the questions, 'When?' 'Where?' and 'How?'

When?

We encountered some of the adjuncts of time at the end of the previous chapter. For example:

*We are going to have a drink together **tomorrow**.*

As well as giving information about the point in time at which something happens, they can also tell us about how long it goes on for (eg 'forever') or how frequently (eg 'often')

Where?

These adverbs tell us about position:

*I'll meet you **here**.*

and direction

*She's gone **away**.*

How?

This is a much larger group of adverbs which tell us about the manner in which something occurred:

*She ate the ice cream **slowly** and **thoughtfully**.*

Many of these adverbs are formed from adjectives by the addition of -ly. Since this is the only 'rule' about adverbs many people learn, it accounts for the misconception some people have that all adverbs end in -ly.

Sentence focus

There is a small, but important, group of adverbs that add to the meaning of the sentence in a different way, by focusing attention on a part of it. For example:

*Katherine, **too**, wanted a second helping.*

***Only** Katherine wanted a second helping.*

In the first of these examples, the adverb 'too' makes it clear that 'Katherine' is being added to the list of those who wanted a second helping. In the second, 'only' has the opposite effect: it separates 'Katherine' from everybody else.

Intensifiers

An important use of focusing adverbs is to alter the meanings of adjectives and other adverbs. We can make them stronger:

*She is **incredibly** intelligent.*

or weaker:

*I feel **slightly** sick.*

or sit on the fence:

*The film was **quite** interesting.*

Whatever effect we achieve, these adverbs are called **intensifiers**. It is possible to pile them up one on top of another, too:

*She is **really rather boringly** beautiful.*

If you use adverbs to intensify adjectives as in the examples above, you are creating **adjective phrases**. So, for example, 'slightly sick' is an adjective phrase. If you intensify adverbs in a similar way, you create an **adverb phrase**. For example:

*The train was travelling **very quickly**.*

Here the intensifier 'very' modifies the adverb 'quickly' to create an adverb phrase 'very quickly'.

Other adverbs

There are two other groups of adverbs that we use to help stick a text together (or, linguistically speaking, 'give it cohesion'). For example, in the middle of an argument you might come across a sentence that begins:

Therefore it makes sense to...

'Therefore' is a ***conjunct.*** It links the present sentence with what has gone before. Other conjuncts are 'however', 'moreover' and 'similarly'. ◀ p64

A ***disjunct,*** on the other hand, makes a comment on part of the text: ◀ p64

Fortunately there was no water in the glass!

Other disjuncts are 'admittedly', 'probably', and 'clearly'.

Prepositional phrases as adverbials

Pretty well all the functions of adverbs that have been described so far can also be done by groups of words that are not themselves adverbs. Compare these pairs of sentences:

*We are going to have a drink together **tomorrow.***
*We are going to have a drink together **at the end of the week.***

*I'll meet you **here.***
*I'll meet you **underneath the clock at Paddington Station.***

*She ate the ice cream **gracefully.***
*She ate the ice cream **like an elderly duchess.***

In each case the single word adverb has been substituted by a phrase of similar meaning. Each of these is a ***prepositional phrase***, so called because it begins with a preposition. Most prepositional phrases, in fact take the form: ◀ p79

PREPOSITION +	NOUN PHRASE
up	the High Street
down	our way

p69 ▶
Prepositions

These small words or word groups get their name because they are positioned before ('pre') a word or group of words. They can consist of one word ('up', 'down', 'in' etc) or two ('out of', 'close to' etc) or more ('as well as', 'in the course of' etc).

Other uses of prepositional phrases

For the sake of completeness, it's worth pointing out that prepositional phrases don't only work as adverbials. They also often form part of other phrases.

In noun phrases

They are often used as modifiers in noun phrases, as in these examples:

*That teacher **from County Durham** is a bit odd.*
*Even fairly **up front capitalists** might be embarrassed by that much money.*

In adjective and adverb phrases

They can also occur in adjective and adverb phrases, particularly those involving comparison:

*It was bigger **than the Eiffel Tower.***
*He was the best **of the bunch.***

8 Real-life sentences

So far we have only dealt with short simple sentences; the analysis in Chapter 4 was based on sentences of no more than four words. Life of course is always more complicated than that. In this chapter we'll apply the ideas introduced so far to longer and more complicated sentences.

Three types of sentence

We can divide *sentences* into three broad groups according to the number of clauses they contain and how these are linked.

◀ p90

Simple sentences

A sentence that consists of just one clause is described as a simple sentence. This does not tell us anything about its length or about the ideas it contains. Both the following examples are simple sentences on the pattern SUBJECT + VERB + OBJECT:

> *I trust him.*

> *Many of the most expert and experienced scientists on both sides of the Channel have not been able to trust the statements of either their own governments or the European Commission on this matter.*

The second sentence **seems** much more complex than the first, but it isn't really. It starts with a long *noun phrase*:

◀ pp33–35, 73–75

> *Many of the most expert and experienced scientists on both sides of the Channel*

This is based on the headword 'scientists'. The object of the sentence is also a long noun phrase based on the headword 'statements'. So the sentence boils down to:

SUBJECT	VERB	OBJECT
scientists	have not been able to trust	statements.

p91 ▶ Compound sentences

The simplest way of joining two clauses is to use 'and'. For example:

I don't trust him and he doesn't trust me.

*Many of the most expert and experienced scientists on both sides of the Channel have not been able to trust the statements of either their own governments or the European Commission on this matter **and** many of the civil servants within their own administrations are not going to trust scientists with an unreliable track record in previous scandals.*

'And' is a conjunction (a term deriving from the Latin for joining two things together). The two items it joins are of equal status in the

p70 ▶ sentence, so it is described as a ***co-ordinating conjunction***. Other similar conjunctions are 'but', 'or' (and 'either...or') and 'then'.

Co-ordinating conjunctions can also be used to join words and phrases. For example:

bread and butter

either their own governments or the European Commission

pp92–96 ▶ Complex sentences

When clauses are linked in a different way we create something called a complex sentence. The term 'complex' describes the grammatical structure and not the length of the sentence or its complexity of meaning.

In a complex sentence, one clause is grammatically superior to the others. This is the **main clause** and other clauses are **subordinate** to it. The best way to show how this works is to take a simple sentence and then turn it into a complex one.

SUBJECT	VERB	COMPLEMENT
Her message	was	tragic.
What she told us	was	tragic.

Here we started with a subject that was a noun phrase and have substituted a clause for it, so that we end up with two clauses. Although a complex sentence has a **main** clause, this does not mean that the main clause is necessarily one that will stand alone if you pull it out of the sentence:

MAIN CLAUSE: (SUBJECT) was tragic.

SUBORDINATE CLAUSE: What she told us

A clause that does the job of a noun phrase as subject, object or complement is a **nominal clause**.

Relative clauses

◀ pp94–95

Noun phrases may contain a clause that modifies the headword. Such clauses are called **relative clauses** and are introduced by the **relative pronouns** 'who(m)', 'which' and 'that'. Again the clause can replace a single word or a phrase:

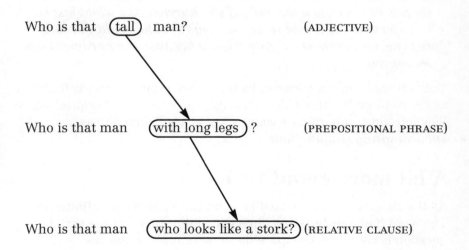

Who is that (tall) man? (ADJECTIVE)

Who is that man (with long legs)? (PREPOSITIONAL PHRASE)

Who is that man (who looks like a stork?) (RELATIVE CLAUSE)

Rather confusingly for foreign learners, relative clauses can also be introduced by a 'zero relative pronoun' – that is to say no relative pronoun at all: 'The book **you lent me** is really interesting.'

p95–96 ▶ ## Adverbial clauses

Adverbial clauses can be regarded in the same way. For example:

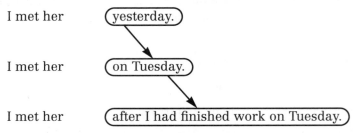

I met her (yesterday.)

I met her (on Tuesday.)

I met her (after I had finished work on Tuesday.)

Adverbial clauses can do all the things that single adverbs can, or phrases (especially prepositional phrases) used as adverbials. The main functions of adverbial clauses are detailed in Section B.

To end this part of the chapter, here is a short piece of text with the adverbial clauses printed in bold.

> ***Although it was the middle of summer***, *Gina felt cold. She wrapped her thin coat round her* ***so that she could benefit from its meagre protection***. ***As she reached the end of the road*** *she saw the bus coming down the road.* ***If she hurried***, *she might just catch it. Unfortunately her skirt was so long* ***that she couldn't really run***. *Several times she nearly tripped* ***because the pavement was so uneven***.

You will notice that a common feature of adverbial clauses is that they are introduced by words like 'although', 'so', 'as', 'if', 'because'. Since they introduce subordinate clauses, these are referred to as

p70 ▶ ***subordinating conjunctions.***

A bit more about verbs

All the clauses we have looked at so far have contained a **finite verb**. The word 'finite' is linked to 'finished' and means that the verb in question is complete. Compare these two simple sentences:

- *Walking on the South Downs in May.*

- *I was walking on the South Downs in May.*

The first 'sentence' is not a complete sentence. It might do as the title for a magazine article, or as part of a set of informal notes. It doesn't, however, provide the kind of complete information that a full sentence does. It prompts the question, 'What about walking in the South Downs in May?'

This is because it does not contain a finite verb. The finite parts of the verb are the present and past tense forms. A finite verb therefore is either in the past tense, or – if in the present – it changes according to the subject in number and person. The -ing participle (eg 'walking') and the -ed participle (eg 'eaten') cannot stand alone as a finite verb.

Where there is more than one verb in the verb phrase, it is the first verb that has to be finite. For example:

*He **was** being told...*
*They **have** been making...*

Verbs are described in detail on pages 60–63 and 76–78 of the reference section.

Non-finite clauses

A clause that contains a finite verb is described as a finite clause. It is possible to have non-finite clauses. These work in a similar way to finite clauses but contain a non-finite verb. For example:

***Walking on the South Downs in May** I met an old farmer.*

The non-finite clause 'Walking on the South Downs in May' could be transformed into 'As I was walking on the South Downs in May...' It is an adverbial clause giving information about time. Other examples and transformations are:

- ***Taken all in all** the results weren't too bad.*
  ***When you take them all in all** the results weren't too bad.*

- *The best thing is **to go there alone**.*
  *The best thing is **if you go there alone**.*

Verbless clauses

It is also possible to have a clause that has no verb at all. You can usually spot these because they are introduced by a subordinating conjunction. For example:

*The meal, **although not very hot**, was perfectly edible.*

Here the clause could be transformed into a finite clause:

***Although the meal was not very hot**, it was perfectly edible.*

Similar verbless clauses and transformations are:

- *The coffee, **when ready**, proved excellent.*
  ***When the coffee was ready**, it proved excellent.*

- ***Even when under considerable suspicion**, the thieves were allowed to circulate freely.*
  ***Even when the thieves were under considerable suspicion**, they were allowed to circulate freely.*

Part B:
Reference grammar

9 Words

pp31–32 ► ## Nouns

Nouns satisfy all or most of these criteria:

- They can be plural or singular:
  *one **cigar**, two **cigars***

- They can stand as the headword of a noun phrase:
  *a **cigar** called Hamlet*

- They can be modified by an adjective:
  *a **large** cigar*

The majority of nouns refer to people, places, things, and ideas.

Categories of nouns

Nouns fall into a range of categories, the most useful of which can be summed up in this simple diagram:

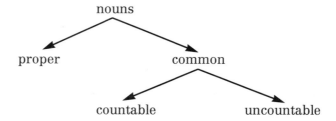

Proper nouns

Proper nouns refer to people, places, things and ideas that are unique. They are written with initial capital letters and include:

- The names of individual people and places (*Jane, Paris).*

- The names of organisations, institutions, publications, films, TV programmes, pieces of music and other things that are unique (*Heinemann, Hamlet*).

- People's titles when used to refer to an individual – with or without their personal name (*the Professor, the President*) – but not when used generically (*some professors, the presidents of several countries*).

Many proper nouns, as in these examples, may consist of more than one word.

Common nouns

All nouns except for proper nouns fall into this group. Common nouns can be countable or uncountable.

Countable and uncountable nouns

Most common nouns have singular and plural forms, because they refer to things that can, in theory at least, be counted. Most English nouns make their plural form by adding -s or -es, and some, like those for words ending in -f, have slightly more complex plural forms. A very small number either have a completely irregular plural form, like *child, mouse* and *woman*, or have the same form for both singular and plural – like *sheep*. A small number of common nouns are not used in the plural because they are regarded as uncountable. Examples of these are:

behaviour	butter	childhood	education
electricity	equipment	existence	health
independence	magic	milk	rain
sleep	technology	weather	work

Clearly a lot of these are abstract nouns, but not all (butter and milk, for example). Some can be used in the plural in special circumstances: *Tesco had several different French **butters** this week*.

Since proper nouns refer to people, places, things and ideas that are unique, they are by definition uncountable.

The distinction between countable and uncountable nouns is important when we decide which determiners to use before them. (See pp73–74.)

pp35–36 ▶ # Adjectives

Attributive

Adjectives help to narrow the meaning of nouns, by giving further information. They are normally used before the noun, which they are said to modify:

> *The union's **new** president spoke next.*

Although adjectives normally come before the noun, they can also come after it:

> *The union's president **elect** spoke next.*

This use is described as **attributive** (the adjectives give information about the attributes of the noun).

Predicative

Adjectives can also be used after verbs such as 'to be' in sentences like this:

> *Peter is **happy**.*

This use is described as **predicative** (since the adjectives form a key part of the predicate of the sentence). Some adjectives can only be used predicatively; for example:

afraid   asleep   alone   content   ready   unable

(So you can't talk about a 'ready car', or an 'alone person'.)

Qualitative and classifying

Most adjectives can be allocated to one of two large groups:

Qualitative adjectives

These refer to a quality that can be attributed to someone or something. For example:

anxious   fresh   simple   young

Classifying adjectives

By contrast, these adjectives allocate things and people to a particular group or class:

annual   British   urban   southern

Grading

Qualitative adjectives can be graded – that is to say you can have more or less of the quality they refer to:

*He's an **extremely** dull speaker!*

The usual way of grading adjectives is by placing an intensifying adverb before the adjective. Common adverbs for this purpose are:

rather   very   extremely   terribly   slightly   somewhat

Classifying adjectives are not normally graded in this way. For example it would not make much sense to say:

*School Speech Days are an **extremely annual** event.*

There are, however, circumstances in which we make such adjectives gradable to achieve a special effect:

*He was **more** British than the British – stiff upper lip and all that.*

Comparison

We can also compare things using adjectives:

*They've moved to a **bigger** house.*
*That's the **most unusual** story I've ever heard.*

Adjectives thus have three forms:

ABSOLUTE	COMPARATIVE	SUPERLATIVE
big	bigger	biggest
unusual	more unusual	most unusual

Adjectives of one syllable and some with two syllables make comparative and superlative forms by adding -*er* and -*est*. Most with two syllables and almost all with three or more syllables use *more* and *most*.

Part B: Reference grammar

pp37–43, 76–78

Verbs

We can classify verbs in this way:

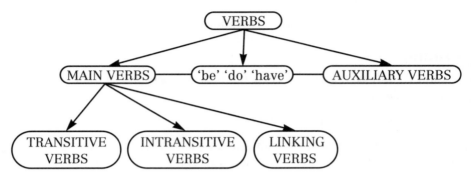

Main verbs

These are also called 'full', or 'lexical' verbs because they are verbs which contain meaning – you can look them up in a dictionary and find a definition. They can appear on their own as the verb in a sentence:

- *My head **aches**.*

- *The Prince **talks** to the trees.*

Types of main verb

Most main verbs can be allocated to one or more of these three groups:

1 **Transitive** verbs

   These are verbs that take an object:

   *She **kicked** the ball.*

   *I **ate** the ice cream.*

2 **Intransitive** verbs

   These are verbs that do not take an object:

   *The prisoner **escaped**.*

   *My tooth **hurts**.*

3 **Linking** verbs

These are verbs which link a subject and its complement:

*You **seem** very happy today.*

*They **appeared** rather unsure of themselves.*

Some verbs can fall into more than one of these groups. For example:

'Are you eating a sweet, Jimmie?" asked the teacher. 'I'm not eating,' the boy replied. (TRANSITIVE and INTRANSITIVE)

and

*Suddenly a ghost **appeared**. It **appeared** rather confused.* (INTRANSITIVE and LINKING)

Auxiliary verbs

As their name suggests, these 'help' the main verb within the sentence, by extending its functions. In these examples, the verb phrase is in bold type and the auxiliary verbs are underlined:

* *They **have been watching** me all day.*

* *By the end of this week I **shall have written** ten thousand words of my first novel.*

* *You **could leave** the difficult stuff until last.*

Auxiliary verbs form two groups:

* The **primary auxiliaries**: *be, have, do*

   Examples of these are:

   *I **am** leaving my husband.*

   *I **have** bought a new car.*

   *I **do** not like the colour red.*

   These three verbs can also occur on their own as main verbs:

   *I **am** very happy.*

   *It **has** three functions.*

   *You **did** a terrible thing.*

- The **modal auxiliaries**: *can/could, will/shall/would/should, may/might, must*

  These verbs are used to build verb phrases which refer to possible events rather than actual events. Compare these pairs of sentences:

- a *She **has visited** her mother today.*
  b *She **might visit** her mother today.*

- a *I **go** to the cinema on Fridays.*
  b *From now on I **shall go** to the cinema on Fridays.*

Inflection

Verbs **inflect**; that is to say that they change their form according to the subject and the sentence in which they are used. They do this in two ways.

Number and person

The form of the verb depends on the subject:

		PRONOUN	*walk*	*be*
SINGULAR	1ST PERSON	I	walk	am
	2ND PERSON	you	walk	are
	3RD PERSON	he/she/it	walks	is
PLURAL	1ST PERSON	we	walk	are
	2ND PERSON	you	walk	are
	3RD PERSON	they	walk	are

We say that the subject and the verb have to 'agree' – you will sometimes see agreement referred to as 'concord'. Failure to make subject and verb agree is a common mistake in writing.

Tense

Many modern grammarians use the word 'tense' in a very narrow way. They use it to mean the way in which the form of the verb is changed to give information about time. In this sense, English only has two tenses, present, and past.

PRESENT	PAST
she walks	she walked
they sing	they sang

There is, however, another way in which the term 'tense' is commonly used. This is explained in detail on pages 77–78. ◀pp77–78

Most English verbs make the past tense by adding -ed to the stem of the verb. A group of commonly used verbs, however, is irregular and has a variety of forms:

PRESENT	PAST
run	ran
hurt	hurt

and so on

Forms of the verb

Verbs appear in a number of different forms:

• **stem**	walk	run	go	swim
• **present participle**	walking	running	going	swimming
• **past participle**	walked	run	gone	swum
• **present tense forms**	walk(s)	run(s)	go(es)	swim(s)
• **past tense form**	walked	ran	went	swam
• **infinitive**	to walk	to run	to go	to swim

As you can see, regular verbs like *walk* form all tenses and participles by adding to the stem. Irregular verbs like *run, go,* and *swim* do not follow this rule.

pp44–47 ► Adverbs

Of all the word classes, the adverb is the most difficult to pin down.
It can occur in many different places and has a very wide range of
meanings. Adverbs can be classified like this:

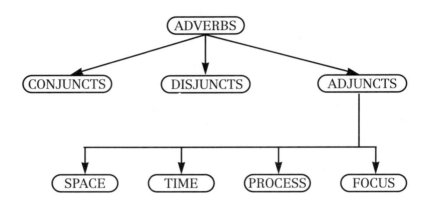

Conjuncts

These are words that serve to link a sentence to what has gone before.
Some of the commonest are:

also	alternatively	besides	finally
first(ly)	however	moreover	next
otherwise	otherwise	similarly	then
therefore			

Disjuncts

Disjuncts don't link the sentence to what has gone before; they
comment on part of the text or the ideas it contains. For example:

admittedly	clearly	fortunately	frankly
generally	incredibly	personally	possibly
probably			

Adjuncts

All other adverbials fall into the much larger class of adjuncts.
Adjuncts 'add' to the meaning of the sentence in one of four ways.

Space

These provide an answer to the question 'Where?' For example:

above	here	inside
there	underneath	backwards

Time

These answer the questions 'When?' 'For how long?' 'How
frequently?' For example:

later	forever	never
often	permanently	yesterday

Process

This group of adjuncts answers the question 'How?' Examples are:

jerkily	sadly	slowly
reverently	well	badly

Focus

As their name suggests, these focus attention on a section of the
sentence. They do this in a variety of ways:

- **to point out that a new item is being added to what has already been said**
  They include:

also	even	too

- **to single something out.**
  These include:

especially	particularly	mainly
merely	only	simply

- **to intensify the meaning of part of the sentence.**
  For example:

very	enough	extremely
quite	rather	somewhat

pp32–33 ▶ # Pronouns

It is often said that pronouns 'stand in for nouns'. While that is true, they also 'stand in for' a number of other grammatical forms. This short paragraph illustrates some of them:

> **It** was raining as Kirstie set out for the nearest railway station. **This** was about a mile away, and **she** was late, so **she** had to hurry, **which** was unfortunate, because **she** had hurt **her** leg the night before.

- The uses of *she* and *her* are examples of a pronoun replacing a **noun**, *Kirstie/Kirstie's*.

- *This*, on the other hand, refers back to a **noun phrase**, *the nearest railway station*.

- *Which* does not refer to any specific grammatical feature, but rather to **a general situation**: the fact that Kirstie had to hurry.

- The initial *It* is an example of a **'dummy subject'** and refers back to nothing at all; instead it looks forward to the rest of the sentence of which it is the subject.

Different types of pronoun

There is a wide range of pronouns available:

Personal pronouns

These refer to people and things:

	SINGULAR		PLURAL	
	SUBJECT	OBJECT	SUBJECT	OBJECT
1ST PERSON	I	me	we	us
2ND PERSON	you	you	you	you
3RD PERSON	he/she/it	him/her/it	they	them

They can be ambiguous if it is not clear to which person or thing they refer. Since English has no general personal pronoun for referring to men and women, some writers have difficulties about whether to use he/him, she/her, or some other form (eg 's/he').

Possessives

There are two types of possessive: possessive pronouns, which can stand on their own (eg *'That book is **mine**.'*) and possessive determiners which come before a noun (eg *'That is **my** book.'*)

POSSESSIVE PRONOUNS	POSSESSIVE DETERMINERS
mine	my
yours	your
his/hers/(its)	his/her/its
ours	our
yours	your
theirs	their

Reflexive pronouns

These allow us to refer back to the subject later in the sentence:

'Mary has hurt herself.'

'I don't, myself, believe it.'

They are formed by adding **-self** to the singular personal pronouns ('myself', 'herself' etc) and **-selves** to the plural ones ('ourselves' etc).

Demonstrative pronouns

this   that   these   those

These help us refer to people or things in terms of space ('that book over there') or within a text or dialogue (*'This is a useful suggestion, but that wasn't.'*)

Indefinite pronouns

someone   somebody   something

anyone   anybody   anything

These are used when you don't want to, or can't, be more precise about the person or thing you are referring to. (*'Anybody can do that.'*)

Interrogative pronouns

who   whom   which   what

These are used for asking questions (*'What have you got on your head?'*) and making exclamations (*'What a lovely hat!'*)

Relative pronouns

who   whom   which   that

These are used to introduce relative clauses (*'The woman **who said she wanted to buy my flat** turned out to be a journalist.'*)

Prepositions

◀ p48

Prepositions can come before:

* a **noun**
  *beyond **hope***

* a **pronoun**
  *after **you***

* an **adjective**
  *in **blue***

* a **noun phrase**
  *after **his last performance***

* a **clause**
  *after **what you have just said***

Common prepositions

The commonest prepositions are:

about	after	as	at	before
between	by	during	for	from
in	into	of	on	over
than	through	to	under	with
within	without			

There are also prepositions which consist of more than one word:

* **two word prepositions**

  according to   out of

* **three word prepositions**

  in line with   on top of

* **four word prepositions**

  by the side of   in the course of

Conjunctions

We use conjunctions to join together two grammatical elements.
A conjunction like 'and' can join two single words:

*You **and** I* know all about that.

or two phrases:

*Your father **and** my mother* have known each other for a long time.

or two clauses:

*I opened the door **and** the dog rushed out of the house.*

Conjunctions can be of two kinds: co-ordinating and subordinating.

p91 ▶ Co-ordinating conjunctions

These join together two items that are of equal grammatical status. In
the examples above, the sentence grammar gives no indication which
of the two things joined by 'and' is more important. The commonest
co-ordinating conjunctions are:

and
but
nor
or
then
yet

pp52 ▶ Subordinating conjunctions

These make it clear that one item is subordinate to the other. They
are dealt with more fully in the section on subordinate clauses on
pp92–93. The commonest are:

after	although	as	because	before
if	in order to	like	since	so that
though	unless	until	when	where
wherever	while			

Like co-ordinating conjunctions, subordinating conjunctions can link words:

*We were happy **if** tired.*

or phrases:

*The scheme was effectively ready **if** rather speculative.*

or clauses:

*It will be too late **if** we delay until tomorrow.*

10 Phrases

Words belonging to certain classes can be built up into larger grammatical units called phrases. For example we can build up a phrase on the word 'dogs' step by step, like this:

I don't like **dogs**.
I don't like *your* **dogs**.
I don't like *your bad-tempered little* **dogs** *with nasty barks*.
and so on.

Each type of phrase is named after the class of word upon which it is based: its headword.

Types of phrase

There are five types of phrase: noun, verb, prepositional, adjective, and adverb.

Noun phrases

These are based on a noun headword and can function as subject, object, or complement of a clause. They can also form part of another phrase.

Verb phrases

These are based on a verb headword. They function as the verb in a clause and consist only of verbs.

Prepositional phrases

These begin with a preposition. They can be the adverbial in a clause and form part of other phrases.

Adjective and adverb phrases

These are based on an adjective and an adverb respectively. Typically, they consist of the headword with one or more modifiers before and/or after it.

Noun phrases

◀ pp33–35

Determiners

Although nouns can stand on their own in a sentence, they often need the support of at least one other word, as can be seen from these incomplete sentences:

… man stood at the bus stop.

… apple was bad.

Neither is grammatically complete. In each case the noun subject needs to be preceded by a word such as 'the', 'a' or 'this'. These, and words like them, make the reference of the noun more precise. This can be seen from these three sentences:

People should be given the vote.

The people should be given the vote.

Some people should be given the vote.

Each has a different meaning because of the word that precedes the noun.

This group of words are called **determiners**. The commonest are:

1 a		an	the	
2 this	that	these	those	
3 my	his	her	etc	
4 which	what	etc		
5 some	any	no	either	neither

There are also determiners which can come before these words. These include:

all	both	half	once
twice	such	many	

For example:

> *All the buses were full.*

There is another group of determiners that come after those in the list. These include cardinal numbers (eg 'seven'), ordinal numbers (eg 'seventh') and other ordinals such as 'last' and 'next'. So, a noun phrase can begin with a string of determiners:

> *All the next seven buses were full.*

Certain determiners are restricted in their use. Numerals, for example cannot be used with uncountable nouns. While we can use 'much/more/most' with both countable and uncountable nouns, the same is not true of 'little/less/least'. These words should only be used with uncountables. With countables the words are 'few/fewer/fewest'. So it's 'less sand' but 'fewer grains of sand'.

Modifiers

Adding one or more determiners is the first step in the construction of a noun phrase. The second is to add or alter the meaning of the noun, by **modifying** it. We can do this by placing words before, or after, the headword: **premodification** and **postmodification**.

Premodifiers

Adjectives are the commonest type of premodifier. For example:

> *an **active** politician*

It is not just adjectives that can be used like this. Nouns can function in a similar way:

> *a **Labour** politician*

and so can parts of verbs:

> *a **serving** politician*

You can even use a noun phrase within a noun phrase:

> *an active serving **'new man'** Labour politician*

Postmodifiers

It is also possible to add words **after** the noun to modify it:

*no politician **today***
(ADVERB)

*no politician **on the Labour side of the House of Commons***
(PREPOSITIONAL PHRASE)

*no politician **who believes in the power of the electorate***
(RELATIVE CLAUSE)

pp37–43, 60–63 ▶
Verb phrases

The grammatical term 'verb' can have two somewhat different meanings. The last chapter (pp60–63) described verbs as a word class. But 'verb' can also refer to a part of a clause. The verb in a clause is sometimes one word, a verb:

- *My head **aches**.*

- *Yesterday the postman **bit** the dog.*

Often, however, the verb in a clause consists of more than one word. For example:

- *They **have been watching** me all day.*

- *By the end of this week I **shall have written** ten thousand words of my first novel.*

Whether the verb in a clause is one word or several, it is more correctly referred to as the verb phrase. Verb phrases can combine main and auxiliary verbs to convey a wide range of meanings.

Aspect

The aspect of the verb phrase gives us information about the nature of the action or state referred to. There are three aspects in English:

1 **Simple**
   *He **reads** the newspaper every day.*
   This contrasts with the other two aspects. They focus attention on a particular feature of the verb phrase in relation to time. The simple aspect is general. In the present tense it is used for habitual actions (as in the example above) and general truths (eg *'When water freezes it solidifies'*).

2 **Continuous (or progressive)**
   *He **is reading** the newspaper now.*
   This is commonly used to focus on the continuous nature of an action: the fact that it went on over a period of time. In the present it is also used to refer to the future when something is planned (eg *'They are visiting Paris tomorrow'*).

3 Perfect

This aspect is generally used to describe actions that have been completed, but the effects of which are, or were, still present in some way at the time referred to:

*He **has read** the newspaper today.*
*When they **had finished** breakfast they left the house.*

English 'tenses'

Some grammarians define a tense as an inflection of the verb – a change you achieve by altering the form of the verb. So, the past tense of 'win' is 'won'. In this sense, English only has two tenses, present and past. But for everyday use – especially by those who are studying foreign languages – this strict definition of tense is not very helpful. There is a broader meaning for the word, which is what will be used here: a form of the verb phrase which gives information about aspect and time. Using the word in its broader sense, English has the following 'tenses':

	PRESENT	PAST	FUTURE
SIMPLE	I see	I saw	I shall see
CONTINUOUS	I am seeing	I was seeing	I shall be seeing
PERFECT	I have seen	I had seen	I shall have seen
PERFECT CONTINUOUS	I have been seeing	I had been seeing	I shall have been seeing

It is this wide variety that makes English tenses so difficult for foreign learners. Whereas French, for example, has only one present tense, 'je vois', English has two, 'I see' and 'I am seeing'. When you add in the vast range of possibilities opened up by modal auxiliaries other than 'shall' and 'will', the scope for sophistication – and confusion – becomes immense:

*She **should have been being seen** by the doctor at the moment.*

Tense and time

The form of the verb phrase is not the only way in which we give information about time. Indeed, English can be rather cavalier about the way in which it applies its tenses. We use the context of the rest of the sentence to supplement or even subvert the tense of the verb. The simple present, for example, can be used to refer to the past:

*This fellow **walks** into a chemist's and **asks** for a pound of potatoes. The chemist **says**...*

The simple present can also refer to the future:

*Next week **is** rather busy. Monday I **fly** to Rome, where I **have** three important meetings. On Tuesday I **go** on to Prague...*

Finite verbs

English speakers sometimes have problems in making sure that a sentence contains a finite verb. A finite verb shows tense. If it is in the present tense it also shows number and person. (This also applies to the past tense of the verb 'to be'.) A simple sentence has to contain a finite verb to be grammatically complete. If there is only one word in the verb phrase, then that must be finite:

- *They went home.* ✔
  They gone home. ✗

If there is more than one word in the verb phrase, then the first word must be finite:

- *The government has been having talks with Sinn Fein.* ✔

- *The government been having talks with Sinn Fein.* ✗

Prepositional phrases

◀ pp47–48

A prepositional phrase is a phrase that begins with a preposition. This can be followed by:

- a noun

  *We met **before <u>Christmas</u>**.*

- a pronoun

  *She was sitting **beside <u>him</u>**.*

- an adjective

  *He was dressed **in <u>green</u>**.*

- a noun phrase

  *That left us **in <u>the worst possible position</u>**.*

- a gerund (the -ing form of the verb used like a noun)

  ***After <u>leaving the party</u>** I went straight home.*

Prepositional phrases can be used in these ways:

- as the adverbial in a clause
  *She was standing **on top of the hill**.*

- as part of a noun phrase
  *The book **on top of that pile** belongs to you.*

- as part of an adjective or adverb phrase
  *The last candidate was **the best of the bunch**.*

Adjective phrases

A group of words built up on an adjective headword forms an adjective phrase. The commonest way in which this is done is to add an intensifying adverb before the adjective to premodify it:

very happy

simply delightful

rather angry

It is also possible to add postmodifiers:

*simple **enough***

*happy **to be able to help***

*angry **about the result***

Adverb phrases

Adverb phrases are formed in a similar way to adjective phrases. They can contain premodifiers:

*The time passed **very** quickly.*

*They were **really** very happy.*
(An intensifying adverb modifying an intensifying adverb modifying an adjective!)

They can also contain postmodifiers:

*The time passed quickly **enough**.*

11 Clauses

Words and phrases are arranged into units called clauses. A single clause can form a simple sentence; two or more clauses can be combined into more complicated sentence constructions. For convenience, all the examples in this chapter take the form of simple sentences, consisting of one clause. They are all **declarative** sentences, the type of sentence we normally use to make statements, since this is the commonest type of sentence. (For more information about sentence types, see Chapter 12 pp89–96.)

Clauses are built up of five basic elements:

- subject
- verb
- object
- complement
- adverbials.

Subject

◀ pp24–25

The subject often tells us what the sentence is about. To do this it has to refer to a person, a thing or an idea. It usually comes at or near the beginning of the clause and before the verb.

What can be a sentence subject?

◀ pp56–57

Sometimes a single noun is enough to do this:

Music can be relaxing.

At other times, the subject has already been defined and we can refer back to it, using a *pronoun*:

◀ pp66–68

Music can be relaxing.
It is less demanding than jogging.

Often we need to define the subject more precisely and so we build on a single noun or pronoun, creating a longer ***noun phrase***:

> ***Some 18th century music*** *can be relaxing.*

Verb

In declarative sentences, the verb normally comes after the subject. The verb in a clause may be one word:

- *The Prince **talks** to the trees.*

Very often, however, the verb in a sentence consists of more than one word. For example:

- *You **could have left** the difficult stuff until last.*

Whether the verb in a sentence is one word or several, it is more correctly referred to as **the verb phrase**.

Object

The object of a sentence normally comes after the verb and refers to someone or something different from the subject:

> *Martin telephoned **his wife**.*

The exception to this is when the object is a reflexive pronoun:

> *Martin hurt **himself**.*

The object may be a single *noun* or *pronoun*, or a *noun phrase*. It may also be an adjective that is being used as a noun:

> *I hate **blue**.*

or a verb gerund (the -ing form, used as a noun):

> *We love **skating**.*

Verbs that take an object are called **transitive verbs**.

Direct and indirect objects

◀ pp26–27

Some verbs can take two objects rather than one. For example:

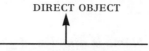

DIRECT OBJECT

The Governors sent Mrs Gray a letter of congratulation.

INDIRECT OBJECT

Structures of this kind can always be recognised, because it is possible to reorder them, using 'to':

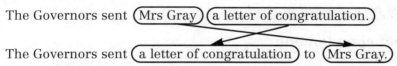

The Governors sent (Mrs Gray) (a letter of congratulation.)

The Governors sent (a letter of congratulation) to (Mrs Gray.)

Complement

◀ pp27–28

The word 'complement' is widely used by grammarians to refer to any grammatical feature which serves to **complete** another. Here, however, it is used in a narrower sense to refer to:

* the **subject complement**

* the **object complement.**

Subject complement

The subject complement comes after the verb and provides more information about the subject. So, the subject and the complement both refer to the same person or thing. Only a small group of verbs, **linking verbs** can be used for this purpose, and they act as a kind of linguistic equals sign:

My mother   is   a musician.

My mother   =   a musician.

By far the commonest linking verb is *be*. Others include *seem, appear, become.*

A complement can be any of the following:

- a noun
  *This is **Peter**.*

- a pronoun
  *The person to blame is **him**.* (Or, if you prefer 'he'.)

- a noun phrase
  *Mr Himmler is **the new Chief Inspector of Schools**.*

- an adjective
  *I feel **blue**.*

- an adjective phrase
  *I am **very pleased to meet you**.*

Object complement

This comes after the object and complements it in sentences like these:

> *The event made him **very happy**.*

> *Yesterday the Governors appointed her **Head of Department**.*

The object complement can be:

- a noun
  *The Board made him **Chairman**.*

- a noun phrase
  *You've just made me **the happiest man in the world**.*

- an adjective
  *The event made her **sad**.*

- an adjective phrase
  *Spurs' late equaliser made Chelsea **sick as a parrot**.*

Adverbials

◄ pp29–30

The adverbial in a clause can be any one of the following:

- a single word, an *adverb*
  *He put the gun **down**.*

◄ pp64–65

- an *adverb phrase*
  *She left **rather unexpectedly**.*

◄ p80

- a *noun phrase*
  *They left **yesterday afternoon**.*

◄ pp33–35, 73–75

- a *prepositional phrase*
  *They were singing **in the rain**.*

◄ pp47–48, 79

Like adverbs, adverbials fall into three broad groups:

- conjuncts

- disjuncts

- adjuncts.

Of these, the adverbials that are most obviously basic clause elements are adjuncts. Adjuncts 'add' to the meaning of the sentence in a number of ways.

Place

Adverbials of place provide answers to questions like 'Where?' 'Whence?/From where?' and 'Whither?/To where?' For example:

all over the place	down the road	in London
in the middle	from the top of the hill	
towards Paris		

Time

Adverbials of time provide answers to the questions 'When?' 'For how long?' 'How frequently?' For example:

at irregular intervals	for several minutes	in 1745
some time last week	twice a year	

Manner

These adverbials answer the question 'How?' For example:

at a fast trot   in a leisurely way   rather jerkily
with tears in her eyes

Purpose

These answer the question 'Why?' For example:

*They were protesting **in the cause of freedom**.*

Reason

These also answer the question 'Why?' For example:

*I couldn't sleep **because of the sounds outside the window**.*

Result

For example:

*The driver lost control of the car **with devastating effect**.*

Condition and concession

For example:

*She was triumphant **although somewhat chastened**.*

Clause patterns

These five clause components can be combined into a small number of basic clause patterns. The first four; subject, verb, object and complement can be combined to make five sentence or clause patterns in which all the components are compulsory: if you remove any of them the sentence becomes grammatically incomplete. They are:

Subject + Verb

SUBJECT	VERB
They	have departed.

Subject + Verb + Object

SUBJECT	VERB	OBJECT
The dog	has bitten	the milkman.

Subject + Verb + Indirect Object + Object

SUBJECT	VERB	INDIRECT OBJECT	DIRECT OBJECT
We	gave	him	a Christmas present.

Subject + Verb + Subject Complement

SUBJECT	VERB	SUBJECT COMPLEMENT
The crash	was	your fault.

Subject + Verb + Object + Object Complement

SUBJECT	VERB	OBJECT	OBJECT COMPLEMENT
The event	made	me	very happy.

There are two patterns in which an adverbial is essential, but they are far less common:

Subject + Verb + Adverbial

SUBJECT	VERB	ADVERBIAL
She	lives	in France.

Subject + Verb + Object + Adverbial

SUBJECT	VERB	OBJECT	ADVERBIAL
He	put	the gun	on the table.

More commonly, however, the adverbial is an optional component and can crop up in many different places:

ADVERBIAL	SUBJECT	VERB
Unfortunately	they	have departed.

SUBJECT	VERB	OBJECT	ADVERBIAL
The dog	has bitten	the milkman	**on the ankle**.

SUBJECT	ADVERBIAL	VERB	OBJECT	OBJECT 2
We	**foolishly**	gave	him	a Christmas present.

SUBJECT	VERB	ADVERBIAL	COMPLEMENT
The crash	was	**partly**	your fault.

SUBJECT	VERB	OBJECT	COMPLEMENT	ADVERBIAL
The event	made	me	very happy	**all day**.

Language creativity

Although the patterns are simple, they form the basis of an infinite variety of clauses. For example:

SUBJECT	VERB	ADVERBIAL
The cat	sat	on the mat.

can be developed into:

The black and white cat with a long tail	might have been sitting	on the brand new mat on the landing.

and has the same pattern as:

My Uncle and Aunt	used to live	in a small bungalow in St Bees.

12 Sentences

Types of sentence

◀ pp23–24

There are four types of sentence:

Declarative

These are sentences normally used to make **statements** like 'Elephants are dangerous'. In declarative sentences the normal word order is to begin with the subject, followed immediately or fairly shortly afterwards by the verb.

Interrogative

These are normally used to ask **questions**. There are three types of interrogative question:

- **yes/no**
  These are question sentences that can normally only be properly answered by 'yes' or 'no'. For example, *'Did you see the lightning last night?'*

- **wh- questions**
  These begin with a question word: 'Who/whom/whose', 'What', 'Which', 'How', 'Why', 'When', 'Where'. They are open questions inviting a wide range of possible answers.

- **either/or**
  Some questions offer the respondent two possible answers. For example: *'Does this book belong to you or Denzil?'*

Imperative

These are normally used to make **commands, orders, requests** etc like *'Look at that elephant!'* They commonly lack a sentence subject, which is assumed to be 'you'.

Exclamative

These are used to make **exclamations** of various kinds. They begin
with 'What' or 'How' and then place the object or the complement
before the subject:

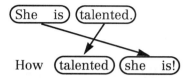

pp49–51 ▶ # Simple and multiple sentences

Sentences can be classified like this:

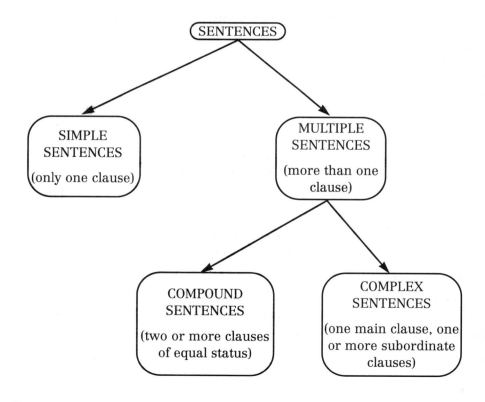

Compound sentences

Much of the time we need to combine clauses in a variety of ways in order to express shades of meaning that are unavailable if we restrict ourselves to simple sentences. At its crudest a succession of simple sentences can have a very childish ring to it:

We got up early. We went in the car. Daddy drove us to the seaside. It was a lovely day. The sun was shining...

At an early age children try to overcome this by stringing longer sentences together using conjunctions such as 'and' and 'then'. They have discovered the simplest way of constructing multiple sentences: building compound sentences.

In a compound sentence we simply bolt clauses together using **co-ordinating conjunctions**

    and   but   nor   or   then   yet

So, these two clauses:

I didn't go to work yesterday
my boss sacked me

Can be combined in a variety of ways:

*I didn't go to work yesterday **and** my boss sacked me.*
*My boss sacked me **and** I didn't go to work yesterday.*
*I didn't go to work yesterday **then** my boss sacked me.*
*I didn't go to work yesterday **but** my boss sacked me.*

As you can see, these conjunctions do not throw much light on the relationship between the two clauses. 'And' just joins them together, although the order in which we place the two clauses affects the meaning; 'then' tells us that one occurred before the other; and 'but' suggests that there is some kind of conflict between the two statements.

Complex sentences

If we want to express anything more sophisticated, we have to adjust the relationship between the two clauses. Instead of the two being of equal grammatical weight, one has to take over control of the sentence; it has to become the **main clause**. The other clause(s) are then **subordinate** to it. In these versions of the sentence, the main clause is printed in bold type:

> ***I didn't go to work yesterday*** *because my boss sacked me.*
> ***My boss sacked me*** *because I didn't go to work yesterday.*
> ***I didn't go to work yesterday*** *so my boss sacked me.*
> ***My boss sacked me*** *so I didn't go to work yesterday.*
> and so on.

If we keep the ideas and language but allow a little more freedom in the forms, we can develop many more possibilities of meaning:

> *If I hadn't gone to work yesterday,* ***my boss would have sacked me.***
> ***I didn't go to work yesterday*** *so that my boss would sack me.*

Complex sentence patterns

Complex sentences follow similar patterns to simple sentences. The difference is that one or more of the components of the main clause becomes a subordinate clause rather than a phrase. So, for example, the subject, object, or complement can be a noun clause instead of a noun phrase:

SUBJECT	VERB	COMPLEMENT
His answer	was	a denial.

MAIN CLAUSE

His answer	was	that he just didn't know.

MAIN CLAUSE — SUBORDINATE CLAUSE

What he told us	was	that he just didn't know.
SUBORDINATE CLAUSE	MAIN CLAUSE	SUBORDINATE CLAUSE

Each subordinate clause itself follows one of the patterns described in Chapter 11 pp87–88:

SUBJECT	VERB	INDIRECT OBJECT	DIRECT OBJECT
he	told	us	what

SUBJECT	ADVERBIAL	VERB	
he	just	didn't know	

Functions of subordinate clauses

Subordinate clauses fulfil three main functions:

- they do the jobs otherwise done by pronouns, nouns, or noun phrases (**nominal clauses**)
- they modify a noun or pronoun (**relative clauses**)
- they act as the adverbial in a clause or sentence (**adverbial clauses**).

Nominal clauses

A nominal clause can:

- be the subject, object, or complement of a clause:
  To lose one parent, Mr Worthing, may be regarded as a misfortune. (SUBJECT)
  I replied that I had no intention of resigning. (OBJECT)
  That is what I mean. (COMPLEMENT)

- form part of a prepositional phrase:

  She is the person in whom I place my trust.

- form part of a noun phrase:

  I don't know where you got the idea that I did it.

- form part of an adjective phrase:

  She was very unhappy that she had not been selected.

Relative clauses

Relative clauses form part of a noun phrase. They modify the headword, coming after it in the phrase:

Do you know   *that person **who is standing in the corner*** ?

`|————————— NOUN PHRASE —————————|`

Relative clauses are introduced by a relative pronoun:

who/whom, which, that

The relative pronoun can be the **subject** of the clause:

*I'm going to catch the next bus **that is going to Clapham.***

It can be its object:

*The last bus **that I saw** was a number 97.*

It can also be preceded by a preposition:

*The person **to whom I was introduced** turned out to be a near-neighbour.*

Relative clauses can also be introduced by no relative pronoun, the 'zero relative pronoun':

*The book **you lent me** is really interesting.*

Restrictive and non-restrictive relative clauses

Relative clauses are often an essential part of the sentence. In this sentence:

*I'm going to catch the next bus **that is going to Clapham.***

we cannot remove the relative clause without drastically changing the meaning of the sentence:

I'm going to catch the next bus.

Such relative clauses are described as 'restrictive' or 'defining'.

Sometimes, however, a relative clause is not essential to the meaning of a sentence and can be removed without loss of essential meaning:

> The bus, **which was travelling rather slowly,** eventually arrived at Clapham.

Such non-restrictive, or non-defining relative clauses are normally:

- enclosed by commas or parentheses
- introduced by 'which', 'who' or 'whom'

Adverbial clauses

Adverbial clauses convey a range of important meanings. When used as adjuncts they can have these functions:

- **Space**
  I left the book **where she could find it easily**.

- **Time**
  When they got home the door was locked.

- **Reason**
  I refused to answer **because it might have incriminated me**.

- **Purpose**
  I left it there **so that you could find it easily**.

- **Result**
  He was always late for work **so he got the sack**.

- **Manner**
  She behaved **as she always does**.

- **Comparison**
  I stayed as long **as I could stand his company**.

- **Concession**
  Although it was raining we decided to go to the cinema.

- **Condition**
  If you see Madge, give her my best wishes.

Conditional clauses

This important group of adverbial clauses deal with situations that are largely or completely hypothetical. They nearly always begin with the word **if**. There are six main kinds of conditional:

1 *If the temperature falls to 0°, water begins to freeze.*
   (GENERAL RULE OR LAW OF NATURE – IT ALWAYS HAPPENS)

2 *If you come over, we'll do some work on those accounts.*
   (OPEN FUTURE CONDITION – IT MAY OR MAY NOT HAPPEN)

3 *If I saw Mrs Thomson I'd give her a piece of my mind.*
   (UNLIKELY FUTURE CONDITION – IT PROBABLY WON'T HAPPEN)

4 *If I were you, I'd forget all about it.*
   (IMPOSSIBLE FUTURE CONDITION – IT COULD NEVER HAPPEN)

5 *If the bank had made an error my accounts would have revealed it.*
   (IMPOSSIBLE PAST CONDITION – IT DIDN'T HAPPEN)

6 *If he had been out in the garden he wouldn't have heard the phone.*
   (UNKNOWN PAST CONDITION – WE DON'T KNOW THE FACTS).

At least this is how the language is supposed to work! There are a lot of native speakers who either do not understand how all these conditional forms work or fail to use them correctly. Which applies to a lot of subordinate clause forms and functions. When someone writes in a childish or over-simplified way it is frequently because they do not have a proper understanding of, or control over, subordination.

G lossary

Adjective
Adjectives help to narrow the meaning of nouns, by giving further information. They are normally used before the noun, which they are said to modify. This attributive use is contrasted with the second main use of adjectives, which is after verbs such as 'to be' when they provide further information about the subject. This use is described as predicative. Adjectives can be qualitative or classifying.

Qualitative adjectives are gradable: they have a comparative and a superlative form (happy – happier – happiest, or excitable – more excitable – most excitable); and they can be modified by adverbs such as 'rather'. Classifying adjectives – like 'unique' – are not normally gradable.

Adjective phrase
A group of words built on an adjective headword is an adjective phrase. The headword can be premodified, typically by an intensifying adverb. It can also be postmodified.

Adverb
A single word that can perform any of the roles of an adverbial. Adverbs also occur in adjective phrases and adverb phrases. They are used to modify the adjective or adverb. They frequently occur before the word they modify (premodification), but some can come after it (postmodification).

Adverbial
An adverbial can be:
- a single adverb
- an adverb phrase (an adverb modified by one or more other adverbs)
- a prepositional phrase
- a noun phrase
- a subordinate clause.

Adverbials can be divided into:
- conjuncts
  These link the sentence to what has gone before.
- disjuncts
  These comment on part of the text.
- adjuncts
  These provide further information about:
  space
  time
  process
  or they focus attention on part of the sentence.

Adverbial clause

Adverbial clauses can express a variety of different meanings:
- place
- time
- reason
- purpose
- result
- concession
- manner
- comparison
- comment
- condition.

Aspect

The verb phrase can have one of three aspects:
- simple (she walks, they walked)
- continuous or progressive (she is walking, they were walking)
- perfect (she has walked, they had walked).

Clause

A grammatical structure that normally contains at least a subject and a verb, and which may contain other components: object, complement, or adverbial or some combination of these. A finite clause contains a finite verb. It is also possible to have non-finite clauses and verbless clauses.

Clause patterns

The five clause components can be arranged into seven basic clause patterns:

SUBJECT+VERB

SUBJECT+VERB+OBJECT

SUBJECT+VERB+INDIRECT OBJECT+DIRECT OBJECT

SUBJECT+VERB+COMPLEMENT

SUBJECT+VERB+OBJECT+ COMPLEMENT

SUBJECT+VERB+ADVERBIAL

SUBJECT+VERB+OBJECT+ADVERBIAL

A single clause may stand alone as a simple sentence. In a sentence with more than one clause, the clauses can be main or subordinate. If you link two main clauses, using a co-ordinating conjunction like 'and', you create a compound sentence. In a complex sentence, on the other hand, there is usually one main clause and one or more subordinate clauses.

Subordinate clauses can be:
- nominal
- relative
- adverbial.

Complement

There are two types of sentence complement:

1 Subject complement

This normally comes after the verb and refers to the same person, thing, or idea as the subject. The verb in such sentences is a linking verb such as 'be', 'seem', or 'appear'.

2 Object complement

Some sentences follow the pattern:

SUBJECT	VERB	OBJECT	COMPLEMENT
They	made	me	captain.

Here the object complement refers to the same person as the object, which it serves to complete.

Complex sentence

In a complex sentence there is a main clause to which the other clause or clauses are subordinate.

Compound sentence

A compound sentence contains two or more grammatically equal clauses called main clauses. They are linked by co-ordinating conjunctions: and, but, nor, or, then, yet.

Conditional

Conditional sentences deal with situations that are – for one reason or another – hypothetical. These range from scientific generalisations through open possibilities to situations that are unlikely, unknown, or impossible.

Descriptive grammar

Descriptive grammar is based on the observation of real language in use and seeks to describe the patterns observed as 'rules'.

Determiner

Determiners come before the headword in the noun phrase and help to determine just what the headword refers to. A wide range of words can act as determiners. The commonest are:

1 articles (a(n)/the)
2 demonstratives (this/that etc)
3 possessive determiners (my/her etc)
4 interrogative determiners (in questions) – which/what etc
5 indefinite determiners (some/any etc).

There are many other determiners and it is possible to have more than one in a noun phrase: 'all their many enemies'.
It is also possible to have a noun phrase in which there is no determiner.

Finite verb

A finite verb shows:
*   tense
*   number
*   person.

If the verb phrase contains more than one word, then it is the first verb that should be finite:

We **have been waiting** for her all day.

Grammar

Grammar is the study of the way in which sentences are constructed and words are changed to fit into them.

Headword

The key word in a phrase which gives that type of phrase its name:

- noun phrase
- verb phrase, etc.

Morphology

Morphology is the study of how the form of words changes according to use – eg the addition of 's' to form a plural.

Nominal clause

Nominal clauses are subordinate clauses that can be:

- subject, object, or complement of a main clause
- part of a prepositional phrase
- part of a noun phrase
- part of an adjective phrase.

Noun

Nouns satisfy all or most of these criteria:

1 They can be plural or singular:
one cigar, two cigars

2 They can stand as the headword of a noun phrase:
a cigar called Hamlet

3 They can be modified by an adjective:
a large cigar

Nouns can be:

- common or proper
Proper nouns are the names of people, places, organisations and works of art, literature, music. All other nouns are common nouns.
- countable or uncountable.

Noun phrase

A noun phrase is a group of words built up on a noun or pronoun, which forms the headword of the phrase. In addition to the headword, there can be any or all of these components:
- determiner
- premodifier
- postmodifier.

DETERMINER	PREMODIFIER	HEADWORD	POSTMODIFIER
that	green	book	of yours

A noun phrase can form the subject, object or complement of a clause; it can also form part of another phrase.

Number and person

In the present tense the form of the verb changes according to number:

he walks, they walk

It also changes according to person:

1st   I walk
2nd you walk
3rd   she walks

Object

The object of the sentence normally comes after the verb. It can be:
- a noun (or an adjective used as a noun)
- a pronoun
- a noun phrase
- a gerund.

The object of a sentence usually refers to a person, thing, or idea different from the subject (unless it is a reflexive pronoun: 'I hurt myself.') Some verbs take two objects, direct and indirect.

Person

See Number

Possessives

See Pronouns

Postmodifier

A modifier that comes after the word it modifies. In a noun phrase postmodifiers include:

- adverbs
- prepositional phrases
- relative clauses.

Premodifier

A modifier that comes before the word it modifies. In an adjective or adverb phrase a typical premodifier is an intensifying adverb like 'very' or 'extremely'.

In a noun phrase premodifiers come between the determiner and the headword. They include:

- adjectives
- nouns
- verbs ending in -ing or -ed
- noun phrases.

Preposition

Prepositions introduce a prepositional phrase and can be followed by:

- a noun
- a pronoun
- a noun phrase
- a gerund
- a clause starting with words like which.

Prepositions may consist of a single word (like 'to', 'from', 'before') or a small group of words (like 'in front of'), in which case they are referred to as compound prepositions.

Prepositional phrase

Prepositional phrases are introduced by a preposition, the headword of the phrase. Prepositional phrases can act as postmodifiers in noun and adjective phrases. They can also act as adverbials in a wide variety of situations.

Pronoun

A class of words that refer back (or, less frequently, forward) to part of the text or an idea contained within it. They fall into a number of groups:

Personal pronouns

	SINGULAR	PLURAL
1ST PERSON	I/me	we/us
2ND PERSON	you	you
3RD PERSON	he/she/him/ her/it/one	they/them

Possessive pronouns
mine, ours etc

Possessive determiners
my, our etc

Reflexive pronouns
myself, ourselves etc

Demonstrative pronouns
this/that/these/those

Interrogative pronouns
who/whom/whose/which/what

Indefinite pronouns
some/someone etc, any/anyone etc
none/no one etc all/everyone etc
either/neither/both/each

Relative clause

Relative clauses postmodify the headword of a noun phrase. They are introduced by relative pronouns: who, whom, whose, that, which; or by no relative pronoun ('The man I met last week is an Italian.')
Relative clauses can contain:
- a finite verb
- an -ing participle
- an -ed participle
- an infinitive.

Relative clauses may be restrictive, in which case their removal would radically alter the meaning of the noun phrase, or non-restrictive, in which case they simply add non-essential information.

Sentence types

There are four communicative purposes for sentences, each of which produces one or more typical grammatical patterns:

- statement
- question
- directive (sometimes called a command)
- exclamation.

Subject

Sentences can be divided into two parts:

- subject
- predicate.

The subject of a sentence can be:

- a noun
- a pronoun
- a noun phrase.

Syntax

Syntax is the study of how words are organised into sentences.

Tense

The word 'tense' can be used in two ways:

- to refer to a verb inflection
  In this sense, English verbs have two tenses, present and past.
- to refer to forms of the verb phrase which give information about time and aspect.

In this sense English has twelve 'tenses' which are listed on page 79.

It is important to distinguish between tense and time. Tense refers to the form of the verb phrase, while time tells us when something happened. Although we use tense to indicate time, we can do this in other ways, and the same tense can be used to refer to a wide range of different times.

Traditional grammar

Traditional grammar was prescriptive and sought to tell people how they should speak and write.

Verb

The word 'verb' is used in two related ways:
- to refer to the verb in sentences, the verb phrase
- to refer to a word class.

Verb as a word class

Verbs can be divided into two groups:

1 Main verbs

These are verbs that have a 'dictionary meaning'. They can stand on their own as the verb phrase. They may be:
- transitive (verbs that take an object)
- intransitive (verbs that do not take an object)
- linking (verbs that are followed by a complement).

2 Auxiliary verbs

These are verbs that work with a main verb to form a verb phrase. They fall into two groups:
- **modal auxiliaries**
  can/could, will/shall/would/should, may/might, must
- **primary verbs**
  be, have, do

These three verbs act us 'pure' auxiliaries, but they can also stand alone as main verbs.

Verbs have five forms or parts:
- stem (walk, go)
- present participle (walking, going)
- past participle (walked, gone)
- present tense (walk/walks, go/goes)
- past tense (walked, went).

See also: finite verb, aspect, tense

Verb phrase

The verb in a sentence is more correctly called the verb phrase. A verb phrase consists of one or more words, all of which must be verbs.
See also: verb, aspect, tense, finite verb

Index

Index

Index

Index